LONG-DISTANCE PARENTING

Other books by the author

WOMEN IN TRANSITION: A Feminist Handbook on Separation and Divorce (co-author)

FOR BETTER, FOR WORSE: A Feminist Handbook on Marriage and Other Options (contributing editor)

CO-PARENTING: Sharing Your Child Equally. A Source Book for the Separated or Divorced Family

JOINT CUSTODY AND CO-PARENTING: Sharing Your Child Equally. A Source Book for the Separated or Divorced Family

LONG-DISTANCE PARENTING

Miriam Galper Cohen

NAL BOOKS

NEW AMERICAN LIBRARY

A DIVISION OF PENGUIN BOOKS USA INC., NEW YORK
PUBLISHED IN CANADA BY
PENGUIN BOOKS CANADA LIMITED, MARKHAM, ONTARIO

NAL TRADEMARK REG. U.S. PAT. OFF. AND FOREIGN COUNTRIES
REGISTERED TRADEMARK—MARCA REGISTRADA
HECHO EN CHICAGO, U.S.A.

SIGNET, SIGNET CLASSIC, MENTOR, ONYX, PLUME,
MERIDIAN and NAL BOOKS are published *in the United States* by
New American Library, a division of Penguin Books USA Inc.,
1633 Broadway, New York, New York 10019, *in Canada* by Penguin
Books Canada Limited, 2801 John Street, Markham, Ontario L3R
1B4

Library of Congress Cataloging-in-Publication Data

Cohen, Miriam Galper, 1940–
Long-distance parenting / by Miriam Galper Cohen
p. cm.
ISBN 0-453-00698-1
1. Parenting, Part-time—United States. 2. Divorced parents—
United States. 3. Children of divorced parents—United States.
I. Title.
HQ755.8.C644 1989
306.874—dc20   89-3439
                                                          CIP

Designed by Leonard Telesca

First Printing, September, 1989

1 2 3 4 5 6 7 8 9

PRINTED IN THE UNITED STATES OF AMERICA

To my husband Herb, who found me across the miles, and to our children, Josh and Satya, who know how it feels to live apart from a parent

Acknowledgments

I am indebted to all the long-distance families—parents, children, and grandparents—who spoke with me about the heartache of being apart and the commitment they have to remain close despite enormous obstacles. Their stories inspired me, often moved me to tears, and are the heart and soul of this book. I sincerely thank them all.

The support and involvement of many people sustained me through the task of writing this book. My long-time, dear friends Carl Hirsch, Alice Matusow, and Carolyn Kott Washburne were with me, as ever. Linda Sterthous edited the first draft of this book and cheered me on. Paula Rosen's support, clinical insight, and technical assistance was invaluable. My colleague, Patricia Bogin Wisch, was always supportive. I am lucky to have them in my life.

Many clinicians shared their thinking with me. Nighttime strolls in the neighborhood with Linda Glaser and talks with Constance Ahrons, Marla Isaacs, Ken Lewis, and Lita Linzer Schwartz were most helpful. I thank my friends and colleagues at the Institute for Comprehensive Family Therapy in Spring House, Pennsylvania, for frequently asking me how the book was coming along. Particular thanks to Molly Layton for her incisive comments and astute clinical thinking. Bea Mueller, Constance Tambourine, and Beth Coltoff offered their special assistance as well.

Thanks to John Tambourine, who brought me into the computer age and whose hotline was always available to me.

Melissa Mandrell was a most reliable, efficient, and competent research associate. My sincere thanks.

Jane Dystel was an agent who didn't take no for an answer. My deepest thanks to her for believing in me, long-distance at that. Alexia Dorszynski, my editor, was extremely helpful throughout the process and encouraged me to keep on writing. She is an editor *par excellence.* Any writer would be fortunate to have her making all those funny little marks on a manuscript.

My ex-husband, Jeff Galper, was especially sensitive to my needs as a long-distance parent. We have continued the partnership of parenting we started so many years ago, co-parenting now across the miles. I want to thank him and his wife, Nicandra, for always welcoming me in their home.

I am extremely grateful to Sam Kirschner for all his teachings.

My sister in spirit, Elaine Radiss, offered her clinical wisdom, encouragement, and friendship on a daily basis. She helped me maintain my sense of humor and promised me it would all be over soon.

My stepdaughter, Satya Cohen, helped me in my early fumblings on the word processor. Her sweet sensitivity taught me a lot.

Josh Galper, my son, provided enthusiastic support from the very beginning of this project. He made long-distance parenting as easy as it could be by being always loving and almost always communicative.

My husband, Herb Cohen, comforted me in my first troubled years as a long-distance parent. In the process of writing this book, he always came through for me. He massaged my neck, offered his perceptive observations on issues I was struggling with, and did the food shopping all year. His love is my foundation.

And finally, my gratitude to my parents, Charlotte and Sirol Katz, who have always been in my corner. They taught me about the importance of contributing to other people's lives and the power of education. I am most appreciative of all their efforts on my behalf.

—Miriam Galper Cohen, M.S.
Glenside, Pennsylvania
February, 1989

Contents

Preface

When my first husband and I divorced many years ago, my greatest fear was that eventually our son would choose to live with his father. I wrote about this issue in an earlier book, *Joint Custody and Co-Parenting*. Ten years later, this fear became a reality. When my son first moved to Vermont to live with his father at age fourteen, I had just remarried and had a new stepdaughter living with us. I should have been happy, but I was not. I was grieving for my son. I cried all the time, or so it seemed to me.

Gradually, I learned how to cope with my loss and make the best of the situation. There is no question that I missed out on the day-to-day joys and responsibilities of raising a child. What I gained, however, was a deeper appreciation of my son and a more intimate relationship with him. Each phone call, letter, and visit became more meaningful. We learned to use each contact to its fullest, communicating our thoughts and feelings to each other.

At about the same time as Josh moved, I began to see families in my family therapy practice who were facing similar issues. I had always specialized in the area of families in transition—families experiencing separation, divorce, remarriage, and stepparenting. My practice began to include children, raised in a variety of custody arrangements, who were now teenagers and wanted a room of their own—*one* room. They were asking to live with one parent, often the same-sex parent. Sometimes this entailed a move many miles away, leaving one parent behind. The family in transition now was making major moves, crossing continents, spanning the globe.

I started to look into my own experience as a long-distance parent more closely and to use this and the experiences of families I was working with to formulate some new thinking on the subject. I began to hear of more and more families with many miles in between a parent and child. Some relationships suffered considerably; others seemed to be managing fairly well, with parents and children forging deep connections with each other across the miles. What made for the difference? Were there rules or techniques that parents could use to stay in touch with their children? How could ex-spouses help or hinder that process? I decided to see for myself.

I wrote a letter to everyone I knew—friends, relatives, colleagues, other therapists, lawyers, etc.—and asked them to provide names of parents who had long-distance relationships with their children after divorce. I also wanted to speak with the local, or custodial parent, as well as with the children and their grandparents. I sent a questionnaire to 225 people and conducted as many interviews as I could, either over the phone or in person. People were extremely willing to participate. Some told heart-rending stories of being out of touch with their children for many years. Others told of being strong in the faith that their love would prevail, no matter what the distance. Mostly, it was the children who told the most poignant accounts of being apart from a parent. Some children were despondent about the separation, but most were optimistic and wanted other kids to know that thinking positively was the best medicine for an aching heart. Everyone was eager to participate, hoping their experiences would benefit someone else.

In order to promote fairness in gender, I have alternately used he's and she's, daughters and sons, and portrayed both mothers and fathers as long-distance parents. For the most part, I have used ex-partner instead of ex-spouse in order to include parents who never married. Except in rare instances, all names have been changed.

Books such as this one are born of personal pain. I

hope that out of my own experiences and the experiences of the families I interviewed, the reader will be able to have more loving and satisfying relationships with their long-distance children.

CHAPTER 1

An Introduction to Long-Distance Parenting

Who is a long-distance parent? A long-distance parent is one who is unable to be involved in his or her child's daily life because of distance, rather than because of a busy schedule or limited visitation rights. A long-distance parent cannot attend PTA meetings or drop over to the ballfield to watch a midweek Little League game. Long-distance parents who live within driving distance might see their children on weekends, but most often it is only on special occasions, such as holidays and vacations, that long-distance parents see their kids.

A long-distance parent is often unavailable in case of emergency. You know what that means. If your daughter is sick, you as the long-distance parent are usually notified, but you can't rush right over to see how she is. When David's daughter broke her leg in a bicycle accident, his ex-wife called him right away.

I felt so helpless. Of course I called my daughter a lot and sent her cards and flowers, but I couldn't be there with her. She told me that she understood, but I felt badly about it for a long time afterward.

You depend on the courtesy and good will of your ex-partner to let you know how things are going. You can't see for yourself; you can't reassure both yourself and your child by your presence. If your ex-partner gets sick, you are not the person called to see if your child can stay with you for a few days. You are not second in command. You can't go to school on a moment's notice and pick up your child because there's been a fire and everyone is being sent home.

The long-distance parent misses out on a lot of the normal demands of parenting. That means you probably also miss seeing your son perform in the school play, or seeing how your daughter looked all dressed up for her first school prom. You rely on after-the-fact reporting from your child or, if you have established a good relationship, from your ex-spouse. While your son might tell you he was lousy in the play and flubbed a few lines, your ex-spouse might report that he was terrific and got a standing ovation. All you know is that you weren't there and you wished you could have been.

Charles's daughter came to visit him at Christmastime and was rehearsing for her part in the play that the community theater group was putting on in the spring. She'd been acting for years, but this was her first starring role. Charles and his daughter had a great time rehearsing her lines, going over them daily.

> I knew all along that I wouldn't get to see her in the actual performance, but what I didn't count on ahead of time was how disappointed I felt on opening night when I was twelve hundred miles away from my budding Broadway star.

Becoming a Long-Distance Parent

How did you come to be a long-distance parent? How did this situation come about? There are many scenarios. A couple in New York separate. They have a six-month-old baby. Finances are tight, so instead of having to maintain a separate household, the wife decides to move back home with her own mother, who lives in western Pennsylvania. The husband stays in New York to maintain his job. In time, they divorce. He calls his former wife to find out how the baby is. Occasionally, he gets a picture in the mail of the daughter he's never really known. As the years go by, he realizes that although he loves his daughter, he has no idea how to establish a relationship with her. And what of that little girl? What is she to think when she barely hears from her father? She gets a letter now and then but she doesn't know what to make of it. The letters pile up in her drawer, unanswered.

Then there's a divorced family with two young children, a son and a daughter. They live full-time with their mother and see their father, who lives across town, on a regular basis. The ex-spouses have put aside their angry feelings and have managed to dissolve the spouse system while maintaining the parent system. They are in fairly good communication with each other regarding the needs of their children. In time, the father is offered a major promotion in his company, which requires him to move fifteen hundred miles away. With much trepidation and anguish, the father decides to move and leaves his children behind. He writes and calls often and manages to visit his kids from time to time. They fly out to see him on some school vacations and for parts of their summer vacations. This father and his children have a sound relationship to build on, and although the distance between them proves difficult at times, they all make the best of the situation.

As the boy becomes an adolescent, he finds himself wanting to spend more time with his father. He gets a summer job in his father's city, and when the school year is about to begin again in September, he announces that he doesn't want to return to his mother's house. He wants to live with his Dad for his last two years of high school. His mother is very upset by the news, although not surprised. Lately, she has felt more and more that she didn't know how to prepare her son for manhood. She is not a strong disciplinarian; she feels that the boy needs more guidance than she was able to provide. She could insist that her son return home, and she is concerned about splitting up her two children, but she believes her son has a right to decide for himself. While she understands and feels that his father's house is a good place for her son to live, she also feels crushed that she is losing her boy. She then becomes the long-distance parent. She described her feelings.

> The hardest part for me was that my son wasn't going to be around anymore. Yes, he was sixteen, but he wasn't fully grown. I raised him for sixteen years and then he was gone and I didn't feel I could hold him back.—Laura

The Child and the Decision to Move

Whose decision is it, anyway, as to where a child of divorced parents will live? Some people feel that a child should not be allowed to make such a decision, because that would be usurping the parental role. Children are not mature enough, this theory holds, to take all the factors into account. One young teenager I know wanted to move to live with her Dad because she didn't like the clothes most of the kids wore at her new high school at home. Clearly, this teenager was too immature to make such a major life decision.

But what about the adolescents who are fairly stable, mature, know their own minds, can weigh all the factors involved and then say they want to move to live with the other parent? A case in point is my own.

My son Josh (of whom you will hear much throughout this book), age seventeen, lives with his father in Burlington, Vermont. I live in Philadelphia. Josh and his father moved there three years ago after ten years of a very successful joint-custody arrangement, wherein my ex-husband and I lived close to each other and shared all the joys and responsibilities of parenting. Our separation agreement stipulated that whoever left Philadelphia left without Josh. There is no accounting for the vagaries of life, however, and when Josh made the decision to move with his dad, it seemed to be a good choice.

Josh had very definite ideas of his own. He wanted an adventure, he was ready to leave Philadelphia, and he wanted to be with his father. I could not imagine forcing Josh to stay with me against his will. What kind of life could we possibly have together under those circumstances?

Legally, I had sole custody. Our joint-custody arrangement was strictly of our own making. I would have been perfectly within my legal rights as the custodial parent to insist that Josh stay with me. "How can you let him go?" people asked me. "Why are you letting him go with his father? Just tell him he has to stay here with you." I did not feel that Josh was mine to let go or not. Looking back over that time, I can see again that Josh made a good choice. He is lucky to have a father who adores him and who is a good role model for him.

What I was left with, aside from my personal pain and loss, was wondering how I was going to remain a parent with so many miles separating us. If I didn't know the daily details of my son's life, how could I stay connected to him? He had been the light of my life for so many years that I could not imagine him being away from me at such a tender age—only 14½. I knew very well that a boy needs his father, but I was also convinced that a boy needs his mother—this mother, me.

I was committed to doing everything I could to stay in close touch with Josh and to support him in his decision to move. Josh had been living in Vermont for about three months when he started to call saying he was unhappy there, that he couldn't find his kind of people, that he had no friends. On occasion I would also hear about a good time he had at school, or that he enjoyed a party he went to.

It occurred to me that Josh was miserable perhaps because he knew that *I* was and thought he should feel the same level of unhappiness as I did out of loyalty, misguided or not. I wrote to him to release him from being unhappy in any way because of me, telling him that I wanted him to plunge into his new life in Vermont. I let him know that sometimes when you leave someone you love, you think you're being disloyal to them if you begin to enjoy yourself where you are. You feel guilty and stop yourself from having a good time. Josh was most appreciative of receiving my letter. He knew just what I was talking about, he said.

Yes, I was very sad about Josh being away from me and I missed him terribly. Still, my overriding concern was that I wanted him to thrive in his new environment.

Staying Involved: The Problems of Long-Distance Parents

Long-distance parents face unique sets of problems that other divorced parents do not. The most crucial concern is how they are going to remain a vital and active presence in their child's life. Some people give up, especially when their child is quite young and living far away, such as the New York father whose little girl lived in western Pennsylvania. How could this father have reacted or behaved any differently? What would you have done in his place?

Many years after his ex-wife and daughter moved away, this father became a client of mine. Vince spoke poignantly of what he could have done to stay in touch with his daughter. He was full of regrets. He saw that he could have arranged his life so that his daughter and his relationship with her were a priority in his life. Vince could have planned his vacations so that he could visit her, especially while she was still very young. He could have spent as much time with her as possible, even though that would have been difficult to arrange. "Instead, I gave up on her and I gave up on myself," he said. "Now she doesn't even know who her father is." As the years went on, Vince knew, he could have called his daughter, written to her, and sent her tapes (see Chapter 3 for other ideas on how to stay in touch). He would have needed the cooperation of his ex-spouse to maintain the relationship, because his daughter was so young when he left her.

The techniques of staying in touch are not important here. Rather, it is the commitment on the part of the father to be a father, even at a distance. If Vince had acted differently, he would have taught his daughter a major lesson in life: that she had a father she could count on and that he went to great lengths to demonstrate his love and caring for her throughout the years. That little girl would then have grown up with a sense that men are trustworthy and that she was not abandoned by her father. Instead, she grew up with a very empty feeling where her father's love should have been.

As a family therapist I have learned that something is better than nothing. Some relationship with a parent is better than none at all. Children have nagging questions about their absent parent. They question their own sense of worth if a parent hasn't shown a minimal interest in them. They wonder what they have done wrong and then begin to assume that they are unworthy of having had a relationship with their other parent. An eleven-year-old girl I know says, "I haven't heard from my Dad in six years. I wonder if he's mad at me for something I did before he left home."

There are some parents who feel they are justified in their absence from a child's life. The circumstances, they say, make it impossible for them to stay in touch with their child. In reality, behind all their rational reasons, these parents may be fearful, worried, afraid of rejection, or perhaps still furious at an ex-spouse and not wanting to deal with him or her. Perhaps they themselves were abandoned by a parent when they were young. They know how much it hurts. All the more reason to do it differently this time.

Mack hadn't been in touch with his son for years. His own dad left him when he was a boy, and Mack swore he would never do anything like that to his children. When he and his wife separated, he just took off. He'd been waiting for the right time to call his son ever since. "It's been killing me for years, but I wanted it to be right when I finally did call my boy again. I finally realized it would never be just right and I better call him now or I wouldn't ever do it."

Mack didn't get the greatest reception, but he didn't get the worst, either. He told his son he was the biggest jerk in the world to let all those years go by without calling.

I missed out on everything and it was there for me to have—a relationship with my son. That was more than I ever had with my father. Maybe there's a chance for us now, but the truth is I'm really not sure. There's an awful lot of hurt there.

Some kind of relationship is better than none for both the parent and the child. The child then doesn't live in a fantasyland about who his parent is, and the parent has a sense of satisfaction and self-worth in knowing that he has made his relationship with his child a priority, even in the face of adversity. Children long for a connection with their parents, and this can remain an unfulfilled yearning well into adulthood.

Many long-distance parent-child relationships are characterized only by geographical distance; many long-distance parents have created joyous, satisfying relationships with their children far away. Such parents know the importance of staying in touch and find creative ways to do that.

When a child is still young, the onus of staying in touch is on the parent. Children cannot be expected to be responsible for reaching out to a parent who lives far away. Beth's parents recently divorced, and she and her dad were moving to a new city while her mom stayed behind. Her mom wrote her a letter, which Beth saved and showed to me recently.

Dearest Beth,
I know that everything is topsy-turvy for you right now
and you have to get used to a whole lot of new things.
One thing that isn't new is my love for you. No matter
what, I will always love you and I will always be your
mom. I will write to you a lot and call you and I want
you to do the same. When things settle down, I'd like
us to have a schedule of when I will call you, so I'll
know for sure that you'll be home. For now, I'll call
you this Sunday morning. Until then, I love you very
much.

Love,
Mom

This letter meant a lot to Beth. It was her connection to
her mom and her concrete proof that her mom was going
to remain an important person in her life.

In Chapter 2, I discuss the parent-child bond in further detail and relate the ways in which long-distance
parenting affects the bonding process.

The Outside World

What kind of explanations do you give people when
they find out you have a child living far away? People
make a lot of assumptions about long-distance parents.
A common one is that if you really cared about your
child, you'd be living close by, regardless of your personal situation. People wonder about the circumstances
that keep you and your child apart, and they wonder what
it must be like for you, especially if you are a mother
away from your child.

Mothers who are long-distance parents are much
more subject than fathers to the judgment that they are
being irresponsible, selfish parents. Why else would a
mother be living apart from her children? Yet the truth
of the matter is that our society is so complex these days,
our lives are so much affected by the consequences of

divorce, of financial uncertainty, of increased mobility, of children actually having and expressing ideas of their own about who and where they want to be, that a mother may not have the sole authority in determining where her child will live.

A mother whose children live with her ex-husband because she feels she cannot financially provide for them is thought of as an unloving mother. "How is that for *you?*" people ask again and again. Cynthia, a long-distance parent for nine years, recalls what it was like for her when her son first began living full time with his dad. It was a subject she tried to avoid when she was out socially. She felt people did not understand her situation, and she knew they were making judgments of her.

> . . . it's not like that anymore. Either people have changed or I have. It seems like it's no big deal now to say that my son lives with his dad. Besides that, I am so proud of my son and our relationship that I don't particularly care what people think.

Nagging questions from outsiders may decrease your own sense of self-worth as a parent. "Did I do the right thing?" you might ask yourself. "Was a good job really worth being away from my kids?" It may not be, but you cannot let yourself get bogged down by the views and intrusions of outsiders who have little knowledge of your personal circumstances. Your task is to work toward being an involved, effective parent—even at a distance.

It is also important to get support from friends, family members, or a professional therapist. A long-distance parent often feels isolated and alone, cut off from a child she loves. Sheila moved back East with her daughter and left her two sons behind with their dad. She spent the next five years as an isolate. She withdrew from the friends and family she had. Even though her daughter was with her, she missed her sons terribly.

* * *

Calling and writing and cross-country visiting never filled up my need to be with them in their day-to-day lives. I was devastated. Eventually, the thing that saved me was that I found a very wonderful therapist who helped me put my life back together. I'm glad I had the good sense to seek her out, and I am still very grateful to her, many years later.

Sometimes you have to force yourself to be with people who understand what you're going through and who can provide you with the emotional support you need.

Healthy Parent-Child Relationships

My goal as a family therapist has always been to promote healthy relationships between parents and children. Over and over again, I have seen the devastating effects on people of unsatisfying or minimal contact with their parents. Sometimes the distance was not the result of divorce. Parents who are in the military, away on assignment, are long-distance parents. So are parents in prison. Parents whose jobs take them away from home for long periods at a time need to pay special attention to the needs of their children at home. Don, a truck driver, is on the road two to three weeks out of every month. He calls his children a few times a week and sends them postcards.

I tell my kids that even though I'm not home to watch over them, I want them to do well and listen to their mother. They know I'm watching over them from the road.—Don

Whatever the reason for long-distance parenting, it's important to recognize that both parents are important to a child's psychological development. Girls need their fathers as well as their mothers; it is important for a daughter to be prized by her father, to get a sense of her own value as a female. Boys need their mothers as well as their fathers to teach them about relationships. Both parents are essential in creating healthy growth and development in a child.

As parents, what matters to us for our own sense of immortality is that our children have adopted our values, our sense of morality, our way of life. We impart our values and character to our children by being affectionate and loving, by having expectations of them, by talking to them about what the important things in life are. Children learn values and morals by watching their parents very closely in every interaction they have.

One long-distance parent I know writes letters to his son that are filled with his "philosophy of life," as he calls it. His letters always include something about what's going on in the world. He'll relate his letter to a newspaper clipping or a magazine article or a TV show. He keeps a copy of these letters so that as his son gets older he'll have a collection of them all in one place.

These letters are my way of making sure my son knows how I feel about things and that I hope as he grows older, my ideas will influence his.—Paul

Be assured that long-distance parents can have a strong influence on their children. Liza, a client of mine, sensed that her long-distance teenage daughter was becoming increasingly depressed. The mother discussed this with her daughter and her ex-husband and felt at a great disadvantage because she was unable to assess the situation firsthand. She thought her daughter needed counseling, then wondered if she wasn't overreacting to the situation because of the distance involved. Her daughter didn't like the idea of counseling one bit, and her ex-husband didn't feel he could force her to get help. Months went by and Liza didn't hear about any improvement in her daughter's behavior or mood.

She was staying to herself a lot and had dropped out of some of her favorite activities. Out of desperation,

I insisted that my ex-husband locate a therapist for my daughter and that he set up an initial appointment, objections or not.

As it turned out, her daughter did not object strongly when the appointment was actually made. She began to see the therapist on a regular basis and within a short period of time she had resumed her social life, expressing renewed enthusiasm for life. What the parent at home wasn't willing to do, or thought he had no recourse to, the long-distance parent accomplished from afar.

Don't underestimate the power of the long-distance parent. During his first summer away, my son Josh decided to take a job picking strawberries at a town two hours from Burlington. His idea was to rent a room and live on his own. Since he was only fifteen and a half, I was aghast and wanted him to have a room in someone's house, where he would be missed if he didn't come home one night. Josh was totally opposed to my idea. His father was neutral at first but I kept insisting that Josh live in a more protective environment. His father realized that I wasn't going to change my mind, and he then made sure Josh got a room with a family. I think that Josh and his dad never did see why I felt so strongly about it, but they were willing to change plans to go along with my wishes, which was just fine with me.

Your Ex-Partner

Your relationship with your ex-spouse will have a major impact on how effective you can be in your role as a long-distance parent. The best possible outcome of your divorce is that you and your ex-partner have a cooperative parenting relationship. You can discuss your child's needs with each other and instead of letting past animosities get in the way, you focus on putting the child's needs first.

An example of cooperative parenting at its best is the following incident: Bobby, age ten, came home from school with a terrible report card. Not only were his grades bad in his major subjects, but he got a few unsatisfactory marks in behavior. His mother, Joan, was very upset. She spoke to Bobby to find out what was going on and let him know in no uncertain terms that she expected a much better report card from him the next time. Then she called two of his teachers and learned that he just wasn't doing his work—no classwork and no homework.

The next thing Joan did was to call Bobby's father, her ex-husband, who lived six hundred miles away. "It would never occur to me not to call him," said Joan. "I wanted him involved in the situation, especially since he and Bobby are quite close." They came up with a strategy that involved daily checks on Joan's part to make sure that Bobby was doing his work. She also planned to call the teachers regularly. His father called him twice a week to exert pressure on Bobby and to check on his progress. "We definitely went into high gear and Bobby had a much better report card from then on. I guess he needed to see us both take charge."

Bobby's parents acted as a team, working in the best interests of their child. They each had a role to play, each could exert influence on the situation, and Bobby knew he was accountable to both parents, even though his dad lived far away.

The worst situation between ex-partners is where one parent denigrates the other in front of the child, where letters from the long-distance parent are torn up and never shown to the child, or where every effort is made to keep the child away from his or her long-distance parent.

Alan, a client of mine for the past year, entered therapy to help him forge new relationships with his grown children. Alan and his ex-wife divorced when his daughters were quite young. When they were nine and eleven, his ex-wife remarried and had the girls take her new husband's name.

I found out about it accidentally and raised hell. My ex-wife told me they were one big happy family now.

I took her word for it and more or less stayed away. She essentially wanted my girls to forget I existed.

The girls are now twenty and twenty-two and Alan is struggling to make up for years of his absence. He admits that he was an absent father even when his daughters were little and they were all living together.

But they are my daughters and I'm trying to make amends. It's the best I can do, given all the mistakes I made earlier in their lives. I hope some day they will forgive me as I am learning to forgive myself.

This, indeed, is a sad state of affairs. It's sad for the custodial, or local, parent to feel so threatened by the long-distance parent, terribly frustrating for the long-distance parent to have such difficulty in even contacting his children, and an emotional disaster for the children. Instead of having a normal childhood, these children are caught up in loyalty issues and wracked with feelings of anger and depression. Despite their mother's desire for them to forget their father, there is no chance of them doing that. Children never forget their parents and they always carry inside them the experience of loss, the experience of being abandoned by a parent. When a child's emotions come unraveled many years later, as they often do, the child is furious with the parent who has prevented a relationship with the long-distance parent and awfully confused about why the parents couldn't have been more reasonable with each other for her sake.

What happens when you don't approve of the parenting job being done at the other end? What can you do about the concerns you have? What if the other parent does not care one bit about what you think and feel?

A long-distance father I spoke with told me that he and his ex-wife always had major differences about how their daughter was being raised and now that they live hundreds of miles apart they can't even discuss those differences without getting into huge fights. Now, his ex-wife doesn't even want to discuss anything with him, and he is left with all kinds of questions about how his daughter is being raised.

Sam describes his ex-wife's attitude toward parenting as laissez-faire. "She gave the kids a lot more freedom than I ever did, so she was the good guy and I was the bad guy," says Sam. "She basically let them do whatever they wanted. My son is grown and out of the house now but my daughter lives with my ex-wife, and I have no idea what goes on."

Sam hopes that his ex-wife has changed. He hopes she knows who his daughter's friends are and if she has any homework and when she'll be home tonight, but he doubts it.

It would make it much easier on me if my ex-wife and I could talk about things. I wouldn't worry so much. I wouldn't be making assumptions about how my daughter lives. My daughter knows that her parents don't get along, and it makes the distance that much harder on her, too.

In Chapter 4, I will discuss in great detail the many varieties in ex-partner relationships and new ways of relating to your ex-partner so that even though you are an ex-partner you need not be an ex-parent.

The Long-Distance Child

Kids ache, too. We've been focusing on the long-distance parent. What about the long distance child?

Melissa, a twelve-year-old girl who lives with her mother in Colorado, is angry about the fact that she misses out on what's going on in her father's life in Boston. "It stinks, it's unfair, and I hate it," she says in no uncertain terms. Yes, she sees her father several times a year and talks to him weekly on the phone, but she is not satisfied. She and her dad had a very close relationship when her parents lived together. In fact, after the divorce and until her dad moved, she spent more than half her time with him. The change has been very disruptive for Melissa. "Maybe I'll go to college in Boston so I can be closer to my dad," Melissa says, "but that's still a lot of years without him."

Airline attendants see many young children traveling to visit their long-distance parents. They see sadness in the leave-takings on one end and excitement in the reunions on the other. In between they see apprehension and confusion in many children as they fly from one parent to the other, confusion that sometimes the parents themselves don't want to see. They may be so caught up in their own anger and sense of loss that they miss noticing the anxieties and sadness that their children experience. And even if they did notice, what could they do about it? In Chapter 5, I will discuss children's needs and how parents can assist them as they try to live their lives between two parents in two different settings.

Reunions and good-byes are the most joyous and the most heartbreaking aspects of long-distance parenting (see Chapter 6). Long-distance parents and children are constantly either recovering after a recent separation from each other or planning for the next visit and eagerly anticipating coming together again. The children have to make the transition between one home and another, between one parent or the other, between one stepfamily or the other. Both parents need to be sensitive to the issues these transitions bring up, both for their children and for themselves.

Connie, a local parent of two boys whose father lives in California, recounts watching her oldest son cry himself to sleep at night for two weeks after he comes home from visiting with his dad. He has a terrible time leaving his father, and the transition to his life back home is a time filled with grief and longing for him. Gradually, he does adjust, but it is not easy for him. Nor is it easy for his father, whose new family in California pulls him in other directions. It seems that everyone in the family re-acts to a visit from his boys.

Everyone in the family, indeed! There may be many people and many personalities to consider. One couple divorces, parents re-marry, bringing stepsiblings into the family and/or having children of their own. Perhaps this second marriage dissolves and a third marriage is created. More stepsiblings, more half-siblings. A child with a long-distance parent has to maneuver through many family systems to find his own place.

Jealousy and competition between family members are facts of life. When your child comes to visit, feelings get ruffled, people feel left out, and you feel caught in the middle. If you are the local parent sending your child off to your ex-partner, you wonder who will take care of your child now that there is a new mate. Remarriage and long-distance parenting are extremely complicated issues. There are ways to handle the complications, however, and in Chapter 7, the problems of stepfamilies and long-distance relationships are discussed.

Achieving a successful long-distance relationship with your child is a task that requires your commitment. You cannot be haphazard about accomplishing your goal. Your relationship with your child demands constancy and continuity. There are many obstacles to overcome; at times the situation will feel impossible to you. You see the pain your child experiences as he prepares to say good-bye to you. Your heart is heavy as you think about the next four months until you see each other again. You wonder if it's even possible to have an intimate relationship with your child when you live so far apart. You may have thoughts of giving up; perhaps you already have separated yourself from your children by more than miles.

In this book, I will share with you how my experiences and the experiences of other long-distance parents have resulted in loving, fulfilling long-distance parent-child relationships. Long-distance parents are often concerned about their loss of power in their children's lives. They feel disenfranchised, that they have lost their voice in how their children are raised. Don't lose your vote! In your relationship with your children, empower them.

Let them know you want to hear from them and that you will be in touch regularly. Tell them you want to know how they feel about their lives—both the happy times and the sad times. Put yourself into your children's lives in a strong, clear manner. Tell them how you feel about your life, about the times you are apart and the times you are together. Your children will gain their own power through their relationship with you. Through your actions, you can enable your children to maintain and strengthen their relationship with you, thus giving you a direct voice in how they are raised.

Whether you are a new long-distance parent, naturally feeling worried, fearful, and anxious about how such an arrangement will work out, or a long-distance parent who is not satisfied with the kind of relationship you now have with your children, this book will assist you in thinking through the issues and taking steps to bring the vision of a dynamic, enduring, close relationship with your children into reality.

CHAPTER 2

The Parent-Child Bond

A child's primary experience of himself is based on his relationship with his parents. Through them, he learns to be who he is. He measures himself against them. Through them, he learns about similarities and differences. He learns about depending on people and about how to relate to others.

A child's relationship with both parents is a living, breathing thing. A child learns resiliency through trust—experiences that she can use out in the world—or she learns that a parent cannot be trusted and she feels that the world is not a safe place. The more interaction the child has with both parents and the more concrete the relationship is, the deeper the child's emotional development will be. If the parent-child interaction is deep, intimate, and rewarding, the child's personal psychological adjustment will be equally well developed.

Long-distance parents are still very much parents, whether they are in active relationships with their children, are minimally involved, or are absent altogether. If you write, call, and visit your child on a regular basis, then your child can have a rich, meaningful experience of you. If you stay away, your child still has an experience of you, albeit one that isn't deep and is filled more with feelings of loss than with feelings of joy. In either case, your role in your child's life has a direct bearing on how well he lives his own life.

Even if the parent has been absent for many years,

even if there isn't physical contact, even with very little communication for large periods of time, there is often an intense desire and curiosity on the part of children and parents alike to get together and to know one another. This is not to say that the child won't feel angry at the parent and resentful that the parent has been gone for so many years.

Even so, there is a need for children to know their parents, good or bad, and for parents to be connected to their children, for better or worse. Without that connection, both parents and children fail to develop a part of themselves. The kind of experiences an adult has in being with his child is important to his own development and provides him with a unique aspect of being an adult. The parent-child bond runs deep. It defies an absence of physical contact and even verbal communication for many years and still allows for a vital connection between parent and child.

Naomi is eight years old. She doesn't see her father often—once a year if that. Naomi's mother, Diana, is baffled as to why Naomi so adores her father. "He has disappointed her, let her down, and ruined so many times together by his drinking. But I know she loves him and feels a closeness to him that she feels for no one else." Naomi gets calls from her father on a regular basis now. They talk on the phone, sometimes for an hour. "She thinks he's funny," says Diana.

Long-distance parents are forced to stretch the boundaries of normal ways of relating to their children. It's not enough to assume that your child will talk to you openly as soon as you pick up the phone. You and your child might need to work together to have more satisfying conversations. (See Chapter 3, "Staying in Touch," for details). But new ways of relating may, in fact, come naturally. Many long-distance parents report feeling closer to their children after the separation takes place. It is almost as if the separation itself forces both parent and child to recognize the extra effort that is required in order to have a meaningful relationship.

My son, Josh, was not a particularly expressive child about his feelings and it was difficult to talk with him over the phone when he was at his dad's house under our joint-custody arrangement. In order to find out what was really going on with him, I'd have to be around him, sometimes sit silently, sometimes probe gently, wait a while—and then the story would start to unfold. As he prepared to move four hundred miles away, I didn't know how I was ever going to stay in touch with him on that deep emotional level, and I was very concerned that our relationship would become more superficial.

Before he left, I told Josh about my concerns and he said he was thinking about that, too. He knew he'd have to make the extra effort to be more communicative. As it turned out, our phone conversations, especially during the first year of our separation, were extremely intimate and revealing. Josh seemed more willing and able to talk deeply with me than he ever had before. He also seemed genuinely interested in me and my life, and so our phone calls were very mutually satisfying.

Ray has been a long-distance father for the past six years. He feels closer to his daughter now than he did when he was living with her. The distance, about a thousand miles, has forced both of them to develop a relationship Ray describes as friends, not just father/daughter. "If you really care about your children and you're a long-distance parent, you won't let a week go by that you don't touch them in some way." Ray believes that as a long-distance parent, you can't maintain contact once a month and expect to know your children and have them feel close to you. He says you have to go beyond the parent-child barrier, to try and touch further into their lives.

You have to get to the child's deeper feelings. Otherwise, you spend every week talking to them and you hear, "I got a new dress today," or "We went to the store." That kind of talk is not gratifying. If you want to stay close to your child you have to get in deeper.

When parents and children live apart from one another, they are forced to find new ways of communicating with each other, new ways of showing their love and caring for one another. Distance forces parents to open their hearts more, to expand their consciousness, so to speak, to make available more of themselves to the child. You will need to be less withholding if you want to maintain a strong connection to your child.

Sixteen months after Isabelle's birth, her parents, Cliff and Marie, split up. They had met and married when Cliff was studying in Amsterdam. Cliff moved in to separate living quarters and maintained daily contact with Isabelle. "For the next eight months," says Cliff, he was uneasy. "The decision to leave Holland and return to the United States was the most painful choice I've ever had to make." He felt he was stagnating there, with a bleak future ahead of him.

Cliff did move back to America, and for the past four years has been a *very* long-distant parent. "My daughter is an integral part of my life, even though I have no say in her upbringing. I feel a strong sense of responsibility toward Isabelle." Cliff spends seven or eight "precious weeks" a year with his daughter. "I see myself as a significant someone in her life and I do all I can to let her know that I am there for her."

The following situation is an unusual one, but it demonstrates the need parents and children have to know one another, despite difficult circumstances. Warren and Vivian never planned to live in the same city; they had been friends for many years when Vivian decided she wanted to have a baby. She asked Warren to be the father, with the full understanding that it would be her baby and that she would raise the child by herself. In the beginning, that was acceptable to Warren. But as seven-year-old Derek has gotten older, Warren wants to have more contact with him and more of a voice in Derek's life. It is becoming increasingly difficult for Warren to be an uninvolved long-distance parent.

It's probably the least desirable of all parenting alternatives. Sometimes I feel shut out living so far away. But I do my best to stay in touch. I know that even though Derek gets angry with me for not being with him more, our relationship is very important to him and to me.

Warren has asked Derek's mother for a joint-custody agreement. That is certainly a far cry from the original arrangement between parents, but one that Warren feels is justified, given his increasing involvement in Derek's life.

A child who has both parents to relate to, whether near or far away, has a distinct psychological advantage over those children who don't. The child then has the diversity of interaction with both parents as well as more experiences with relating to the two people with whom he has been most connected to from birth and with whom there is a deep psychological bond. Having two available role models, one of each gender, gives the child a well-rounded psychological view of the world.

Parenting Roles and the Long-Distance Parent

In recent years, we have learned that both fathers and mothers contribute in equal importance to the development of their children and that both have a crucial role to play in the healthy development of their children. We know that fathers can be nurturing and actively involved with their children. Samuel Osherson, in *Finding Our Fathers,* talks about men "locating and actualizing the nurturer within" when they become fathers. Similarly, mothers can work outside the home and contribute financially, as well as emotionally, to the family. Sex roles are no longer as stereotyped as they once were and have changed dramatically in recent years. We now acknowledge that both parents have something to offer their children.

We learn about being parents from the way our parents raised us. How we raise our children has a direct bearing on how they will raise their children. A boy who has no image of his father has no model on which to draw when he becomes a father.

In families, we often see a repetition of certain patterns. People may not have control over these patterns, which continue because they remain on an unconscious level. An adult who was left at a very young age doesn't consciously remember his own father deserting him. He will usually say he was too young to remember. Little children do know, however, when they have been abandoned. They might not have a language to express it, but they do experience the loss. Early childhood experiences are deeply etched into our hearts.

A long-distance father's relationship with his daughter will have an impact on the kind of man with whom she becomes involved. A girl who has an adoring father will look for a man who will continue to adore her. A girl whose father keeps himself emotionally as well as geographically distant from her will marry a man who will not be available to her emotionally. She will learn not to expect much from men; she may even shut men out of her emotional life. A girl needs her experiences with her father so that she will know about male-female relationships later in life. If a girl is raised without a father, it is likely that she will repeat this pattern and take total control of parenting as her mother did.

A long-distance father can teach his daughter about ambition, about going beyond where *he* is in life, about being successful. John has been a long-distance father for the past five years. He is very involved in his daughter's life, especially in the area of education. He talks to her about the importance of doing well in school and learning as much as she can. "Her only job right now is to have fun, learn, and do the best she can. I'm not asking her to be the best. I'm asking her to be the best she can be.'' When they talk on the phone, Vanessa, now seventeen, tells her dad about her grades and about her projects and activities at school. ''I want her to have more education than I ever did,'' says John. ''I tell her how bright she is and that the world is waiting for her.''

Fathers need to teach their daughters self-reliance, independence, courage, and how to deal with the outside world effectively. They need to help their daughters feel good about themselves as females. As Linda Schierse Leonard states in her book *The Wounded Women,* ''. . . if a father is not there for his daughter in a committed and responsible way, encouraging the development of her intellectual, professional and spiritual side and valuing the uniqueness of her femininity, there results an injury to the daughter's feminine spirit.'' Fathers can also facilitate a positive relationship between mothers and daughters. A long-distance father can promote a healthy relationship by encouraging his daughter to talk to her mother and not to withdraw when there are difficulties. He can support this relationship by not denigrating the mother in front of the daughter.

A long-distance father teaches his son about how to be a man in the world. A father can teach his son that he can remain emotionally and financially responsible for his family even from a distance. A father teaches his son that being a man doesn't mean disappearing or withdrawing when times get rough, that even though a marriage may break up, the father can keep his commitments to his children.

A boy needs to know that his father is very, very proud of him. Such approval means everything in the world to a boy.

> When my team won the soccer championship, I called my dad right up. He was at work, but I knew he'd want to know. He always wants to know when something good happens to me.—Brian, age eight

Historically, men's options for communicating with their children have been limited. Fathers play ball with their sons, take them fishing. Fathers and sons traditionally do physical things together; a father disciplines his son, teaches him to use tools. How then does a father communicate with a son when he lives many miles away?

Brad lives 650 miles away from his six-year-old son and sees him about once a month. As soon as they see each other, "we're on the floor, wrestling, rolling around, immediately touching each other. I try to hold him and handle him a lot." In between visits, Brad talks to his son on the phone about playing baseball and shows on TV they watch together. "I'm a physical kind of guy, I guess. I don't say 'I love you' but I'm sure my son knows how I feel. We have a special thing going. I can't explain it."

A father can also *say* "I love you;" he can hold his son in tender ways, or allow his son to cry in his arms and share his own vulnerability.

I've let my son know how painful it is for me to be away from him. He's seen me cry, especially when he's leaving and I know I won't see him again for four months. It breaks me up inside. I can't hide those feelings from him. Why should I?—Barry

If a father is emotionally available to his son, the boy can then shift his primary identification from his mother to his father, which is an emotionally healthy move for a boy to make. For a son to form his own identity, he must identify with his father.

What about long-distance mothers, who are increasing in number? What do they teach their children? Mothers teach their daughters about trust, about warmth, about sensitivity. There is often a strong identification between daughters and their long-distance mothers. The emotional relationship is intense even across the miles. In her book *In A Different Voice*, Carol Gilligan describes how a basic identity for girls comes from experiencing themselves as like their mothers. Satya, age fifteen, is my stepdaughter. She lives with me and her father in Philadelphia; her mother lives in California. "I see my mom two times a year," says Satya. "My mom and I argue a lot. Her views on things are different than mine. Still, she knows me. I'm her daughter."

Mothers and daughters have an easier time talking about sex and about boys than do fathers and daughters. And mothers teach their daughters about being competent in the world, about how to use their power effectively. Erin, age eleven, hasn't lived with her mother since she was five. "The one thing she's always talked to me about is that I should be somebody in my own right and not just depend on a man." Erin's mother never finished college and has always told Erin she was going to make sure that Erin goes to college so she can earn a good living.

That's one of the reasons we're apart now—money. She doesn't have the money to take care of me. My mom always tells me I can have what I want in this world if I'm smart. I'm not sure what she means by that, but she keeps telling me she's going to teach me, so I'm not worried.

Many long-distance mothers of adolescent boys go through an awful time as their sons begin to gravitate toward their fathers and express a desire to live with them. Yet, long-distance mothers and sons can and often do remain passionate about each other. It is as if they are having an intense love affair with one another, one that is hard to describe and difficult to understand without experiencing it firsthand.

Vicki and her son Gabe, age fifteen, live 160 miles apart. She had a very difficult time accepting her son's decision to live with his father, but during the past three years of their separation, their relationship has grown closer. "I feel he appreciates me more and has forgiven me for divorcing his father. My son told me a while ago, 'I've looked around and I haven't seen any mothers better

than you.' That made me feel so wonderful," says Vicki.
"I know there is a strong bond between us."

Opposite-sex parents value, prize, and nurture their
children, as well as provide a model for how to be in
relationships. Same-sex parents provide a model for their
children of a way they can be out in the world, as well
as prize them. When children understand the other gender, they feel wonderful about their own.

More Is Better

More is better. Two parents who give the child unconditional love are better than one. Two parents who
care deeply about the child's growth and development are
better than one. Who else cares as much about the child's
successes and about the cute little remarks he makes?
When divorced parents have a friendly relationship, they
can share with each other the special things their child
said and did when he wasn't with the other parent. That
way, one parent doesn't miss out on as much. (No one
else *really* appreciates those little remarks anyway.) And
then you can share your pride in your child together. A
long-distance parent, especially, thrives on hearing as
much as possible about a distant child.

Much has been written recently about the need for
children to have a close, ongoing relationship with both
parents after divorce. Wallerstein and Kelly, in their book
Surviving the Breakup, talk about the importance to children of maintaining contact with both parents. Their five-
year, long-term study on children of divorce discusses the
quality of the relationship with *both* parents as one of the
most significant determinants of a child's healthy adjustment to divorce. "The father's abandonment, relative absence, infrequent or irregular appearance or general
unreliability, which disappointed the child repeatedly,
usually led the child to feel rejected or rebuffed and low-
ered the child's self-esteem." The children who fared

well were those who had a continuing stable relationship with both parents over the years.

When Ex-Partners Don't Get Along

Another important variable in the child's successful adjustment to divorce is the relationship between ex-partners. This is especially true for children who have a long-distance parent. The relationship between parents has a considerable effect on the bond the child has with the absent parent; although children have a fundamental need for a deep attachment with both parents, this need may be thwarted by an uncooperative, angry custodial parent.

"Children are little pirates," says Marla Isaacs, Ph.D., co-author of *The Difficult Divorce* and former director of the Families of Divorce Project at the Philadelphia Child Guidance Clinic. "They go where the bounty is greater." If a father is not actively involved in his child's life, the child's well-being is based on the parent he is living with. If his custodial parent—his primary caretaker—doesn't like the long-distance parent, the child is in a terrible bind. His very well-being is so tied up with the person caring for him on a daily basis. How can he connect with his absent parent, knowing that will make the parent he lives with angry? If Mom speaks badly about Dad and Dad is not there to defend himself, how will a strong bond develop between the long-distance parent and child? This puts an added strain and pressure on an already delicate situation. In Chapter 4, I will discuss in greater detail the relationship between the parents and how this affects the long-distance parent and child.

An absent parent always means something to a child. A little girl whose father is away will have some explanation for herself of why this is so. She imagines she is not good enough, not cute enough, not lovable, or that she is lacking in some way. And children explain a parent's absence to themselves in a very personal way. A boy may decide his father was not proud of him and that's why he's away.

If a father leaves when a child is very young and there is no further contact, the child gets caught in primitive feelings of loss and grief she experienced as a child and carries them into her adulthood. Without contact there is little chance for resolution. The relationship and the feelings connected with it don't get developed any further. She is now an adult walking around with an upset little girl inside her. She has learned not to trust people, not to depend on anyone. Her experiences with relationships are fleeting. As an adult, she will either become very insecure and dependent in her relationships, or she will build a wall to protect herself from ever experiencing that abandonment again. She will not look to anyone else to comfort her, but feels she will have to take care of herself. Either way, her relationships are formed out of the context of being left as a child. Both responses are incomplete and unsatisfying.

Mandy came in to therapy because she became extremely depressed after she and her husband divorced. Although she was very protective of her children, she felt she wasn't being a good mother. Her ex-husband had moved to take a better job and was minimally involved with the kids. Mandy said that she never did feel that close to her husband and was not too sad to see him leave. "I never really depended on him for anything except money," she said.

Mandy's father had left the family when she was four years old. She saw him only three times during her childhood and remembers every visit in great detail. Mandy said:

I missed him so much I could just cry thinking about it. My mother told me to stop crying and forget about him. She said he was no good and would never amount to much. I guess he didn't, but he was my father. I still miss him.

In therapy, Mandy is learning about her relationship with her absent father and how that influenced her in choosing a husband. She repeated the pattern she learned from her parents—men are not to be trusted. They leave home and leave the children behind.

Mandy doesn't want her children to suffer the way she has. She has talked to her ex-husband about how important he is to the children and said that she will help him stay in touch with them. He has responded positively and is making plans to have the children fly out to visit him. He always thought Mandy didn't want him to be involved with the kids, whether he was living at home or far away. She had always told him she could manage by herself.

When a parent is absent, the child suffers. When a parent cuts himself off from a child, a piece of that child's experience is missing. But perhaps you, as a long-distance parent, have questioned the importance of your role. Why bother, you might wonder. Why bother trying to stay in touch with a child who lives hundreds or perhaps even thousands of miles away and whose custodial parent may not be particularly excited about your involvement in your child's life?

Perhaps you reason, you and your child and certainly your ex-partner would be better off if you just forgot the whole thing. Forget that you have a child, forget that you ever had a partner, and get on with the business of starting your life over. After a divorce, people do that all the time. They start a new life. They might remarry, move to a new geographical area, and have a second family. Unless a conscious effort is made to remember the children from the first family, there is less and less communication with them, less and less contact, less and less commitment to those prior relationships. You may love your child but feel that circumstances have forced you to be cut off from your child's daily life. One man I know whose four-year-old daughter lives in Germany is contemplating trying to forget that he ever had a daughter. He wonders how his child could possibly know him, given that he left Germany and returned to the United States when she was very young and given that his ex-wife wants little to do with him. He wonders whether he wouldn't cause his daughter—and himself—more pain if he tried to maintain a relationship. Perhaps his daughter would be better off if she didn't remember he existed and didn't long to see him.

The trouble with this line of thinking is that children *always* long for an absent parent. Parents feel the same way. If you know that somewhere there is a child who belongs to you, you never feel whole about yourself and your life. You know there is a missing piece of you out there in the universe and even if you try to bury your own pain and longing, it never really goes away.

Leo hasn't seen his son, Teddy, for four years now, and it was eight years before that. Leo left his son when Teddy was six years old, and he thought he had a good reason to do what he did. Leo has very vivid memories of the times he and Teddy did have together, the games they played. He thought they were close. Now he is making every attempt he can to get in touch with his son. Letters are not answered, but Leo keeps writing. He even wonders whether the letters are being received.

I don't want my son to have to do what I did, which was to search out my own father when I was thirty years old. He left me when I was not quite two.

Other parents have reported to me that they have been separated from their children for between five and ten years, with minimal, if any, contact between them. Then, when they did want to reestablish contact, they were amazed at how responsive their children were to meeting with them.

Victor hadn't seen his daughter, Celeste, for thirteen years. His ex-wife made it impossible for him and he gave up. When he entered therapy recently about some other issues and his therapist discovered he had a daughter, he began reexamining his relationship with her. Celeste was in college now, so he could reach her without having to speak with his ex-wife. Victor was afraid to call after so many years. He was afraid she'd hang up on him. After many months of soul-searching, he finally did call.

It was like she was just waiting for me to call. We got together and had a lot to talk about, right off the bat. My therapist prepared me for the worst, to expect her anger and rage and to just listen to it. Maybe that will still happen, but she seemed fairly calm and pleased to see me. I really couldn't believe it.

Celeste may have met with her father only out of curiosity. She remembers a man whose lap she used to sit on when she was a little girl—but that was many years ago. She knows her parents fought a lot. What she really remembers is that she didn't see her daddy much any more. She did her best to forget about him. Every once in a while, she'd smell a man with her daddy's smell and she would feel very sad. It may be that Victor and his daughter will not be able to reunite in a deep, emotional sense, or if they do, that it will take years to reestablish their relationship.

Suzanne left her two small daughters when they were seven and four years old. She and her husband divorced and she didn't feel she could provide for her daughters materially. Her ex-husband was "very comfortable" financially. It did not occur to her then to use the courts to get child support, so that she could be a mother to her children. She sees now that she needed a mother herself. She was unable to take care of herself emotionally and therefore certainly wasn't equipped to take care of her children. Suzanne stayed in touch with her children, but as the years went by, they lost interest in her and she gave up trying to maintain the relationship. Her daughters are now teenagers and she is trying to reestablish contact with them. The older daughter has rejected Suzanne, just as she herself was rejected as a child; the younger one will talk to her, but is always angry.

In their book *Mothers Without Custody,* Geoffrey L. Greif and Mary S. Pabst cite money as the major reason mothers gave for giving up custody. Other reasons cited most often were that the children chose the father as parent, discipline problems, to allow children geographic stability, and that the mother was emotionally unstable.

Whatever their reasons for not staying in touch, some parents abandon their children after divorce. There is no mistaking the pain the children have felt over the years. Their parents, too, have been troubled. Leo, who is now in therapy with me, is beginning to wonder how close he was to his son, or allowed him to be, if he could leave him and not be in touch for years. Perhaps his casual attitude about leaving his son is Leo's way to mask his own pain about being abandoned by his father.

Reuniting

If these formerly absent parents are to reunite with their children, they will need to listen to the pain and the loss that these children experienced. Suzanne is tired of hearing about how angry her daughter is, but yet that is what the relationship consists of right now—and Suzanne wants a relationship. She is the parent, and it is up to her to renew the relationship, even if that means experiencing her daughter's anger and feelings of rejection. If Suzanne is to stay involved in her daughter's life, she will need to be in contact with her on a regular basis, even when the conversations are painful. If there is a vagueness or uncertainty about when the next contact will be, her daughter will revert to a relationship based on fantasy.

"The absent parent is either idealized or denigrated," says Molly Layton, Ph.D., an expert in the field of parent-child relationships. "The parent is such a powerful figure in the archetype of the mind," Dr. Layton says, "so that the parent's role is of enormous importance to the child." Dr. Sam Kirschner, coauthor of

Comprehensive Family Therapy and director emeritus of the Institute for Comprehensive Family Therapy in Spring House, Pennsylvania, believes that to maintain the connection with the child is the charge for the long-distance parent. No matter what the obstacles are, if *some* connection is maintained, if a parent can influence the child in *some* way, if any relationship exists between parent and child, that allows for all sorts of possibilities in the future. "By maintaining contact in whatever way you can, by keeping the door open, by letting your child know you care, you are seeding for the future, seeding for a whole range of possibilities," Dr. Kirschner says. Perhaps your child will go to college where you live, perhaps she will go into business with you. Perhaps your daughter's new husband's family lives near you. Who knows what the future will bring?

As a long-distance parent, you must hold your relationship with your child as a high priority. Stretch yourself to maintain a close connection even if there are obstacles and major difficulties to overcome. You will be rewarded by a meaningful relationship with your child. This reward may not be forthcoming immediately, especially if one of the difficulties you have to overcome is an uncooperative relationship with your ex-partner and you don't have easy access to your child. But your child will know that you care, and in time, there will be a sense of coming home for the two of you. There will be a time for you to come together, share your experiences of being apart, your memories of the times you were together and what the future holds for the two of you. The bond between parent and child is a very strong one, and with the proper nurturing it can thrive, even across the miles.

CHAPTER 3

Staying in Touch

How to maintain the bond? Stay in touch regularly. Don't let other things get in the way of a three-minute phone call. Make the relationship a priority even if it hurts.—Max

Max calls his nine-year-old son, Tommy, every day. When his son and ex-wife moved away four years ago, Max decided that he wanted to continue to know Tommy and be aware of his daily activities. Max's relationship with his son involves a major commitment on his part, even though he has since re-married and has two step-children living with him. He writes cards and letters to Tommy, who stays at his house regularly. And Max does everything he can to keep his relationship with his son a thriving one.

What are you willing to do? What *can* you do?

Before answering these questions, you must take a look at your commitment to your relationship with your long-distance children. Ask yourself what you have done in the past to keep that relationship alive. If you are not satisfied with the relationship you have presently, you need to examine the situation and investigate the obstacles. Perhaps it is too painful for you to hear your kids' voices and you find yourself avoiding calling them. Perhaps you are afraid that your child's other parent will hang up on you. But if you tell your children you'll call them and then you don't follow through, you need to stop promising them that you'll call.

Being a long-distance parent need not be an all-or-nothing situation. It's not a question of calling daily or not at all, or doing everything in your power to stay as close to your child as you can (including devoting all your financial resources to this endeavor), or keeping visits and expenses to a bare minimum. You need to find what the right balance is for you, and this will probably take some time to figure out.

The main ingredient in being a successful long-distance parent is continuity. Your child needs to know when he will hear from you again, when he will see you again. A regularly scheduled time for a telephone call means a lot to a child: "Be at the phone on Sunday morning, ten sharp!" Your child will look forward to your call.

You can gradually educate your child about the components for a good phone call. Tell your child to keep a list of the things he wants to talk to you about, and do the same thing yourself. Build on past discussions, talk about ongoing projects, sports events, practice for the school play. You need to know what's going on in your child's life in order to ask good questions.

MOM: Any new projects going on in school?
SON: No, nothing much.
MOM: How did you make out in soccer this week?
SON: Okay.
MOM: You don't sound like you want to talk to me.
SON: Mom, this isn't a good time. There's a show I have to watch on TV for school. Can you call me back later?
MOM: Sure I can. But first tell me the TV show so I can watch it, too.

In the phone call that followed, Mom was sure to talk with her son about the TV show. She was now aware of a topic he was studying in school and could participate in the project with him. If the topic is of special interest to her son, Mom could get him additional information, sending him any books or articles she might have on the subject. Listen to your child, though, and don't be overly enthusiastic when your child isn't particularly interested.

Mark vividly remembers the first few phone calls he had with his daughter after he moved away. They were terrible, and Mark recalls feeling bereft when he got off the phone. Neither he nor his ten-year-old daughter knew what to say to each other. They exchanged pleasantries that seemed meaningless. "I kept asking her how she was and she kept saying she was fine. She wasn't fine and I wasn't fine at all." Several months of unsatisfying phone calls went by before they got into the swing of things. "We finally did learn that we needed to talk about the details of our lives," says Mark. "Also, and I think this is most important, we learned to talk about feelings."

Obviously, it's important for parents and children to keep each other up to date on the events of their daily lives. A different type of involvement is required for conversations that are meaningful and have some depth. Don't expect this to happen in the early stages of your long-distance relationship. But do work toward this goal by educating yourself and your child about how to achieve this.

Of course, the quality of your conversations will depend on the age of your child. A four-year-old will not be as conversant with you about the events of his day as an older child will be. But you can and should ask a young child how he feels about things. Then you must be willing to listen.

DAD: Hi, son, how are you?
SON: Fine, Dad.
DAD: Are you really fine? You sound kind of blue.
SON: Blue? No, why would I be blue?
DAD: Well, maybe it's because we're far apart. I feel blue because of that. I miss you a lot.
SON: You do? Well, I miss you too, Dad.

Audrey describes her first phone conversation with her four-year-old daughter, after she left her with her father. She recalls being beside herself with grief. "I told her I missed her and I asked her if she missed me. She said she hated me and said she never wanted to talk to me again." It was all Audrey could do not to fall apart and to call her back a few days later. What Audrey could have done was to tell her daughter that she knew she was angry because Audrey left and that Audrey understood why she felt that way. Audrey did manage to have a similar conversation with her daughter a few days later and many subsequent phone calls were devoted to discussion of her daughter's anger and sadness about her mommy leaving her. Audrey has always encouraged her daughter to tell her the truth. "My little girl puts her feelings right out on the table," says Audrey. "I always know where she stands, and we have a close relationship because of that."

It takes time to cultivate a relationship in which feelings are easily expressed and accepted. Your relationship with your child before you left the area will definitely influence the kind of long-distance relationship you have. But even a relationship that was distant when parent and child were living together or nearby can become close when they are living apart. It is up to you, as the long-distance parent, to think about your child, her personality and her interests, and then use that information to plan wisely how you will maintain a strong relationship with her.

In the following sections, you will read about how your child's age affects the methods you use to stay in touch. Whatever your child's age, read the entire section because you may find some ideas that are helpful to you throughout.

From Birth to Four Years

If you have a very young long-distance child, you will have to work especially hard to be an important person in your child's life. If you have lived in the same house with your child for several years, this task will be easier for you, since your child will know who you are. You may, however, have become a long-distance parent while your child was a toddler, or even younger. This means that it is unlikely that a strong bond has been established. Therefore, you will need to intensify your long-distance efforts in order to develop that bond. This is critical for the healthy psychological development of your child.

The younger the child at the time of your separation from her, the greater the loss for the child. Very young children need to be given a sense of trust and security in their world in order for them to feel safe. The greater the continuity and strength of their contact with you, the greater will be the child's ability to know herself and relate adequately in the world.

Children feel connected to themselves when they are connected to someone else, or have bonded. The absent parent has to come up with creative ways to develop and maintain that bond with the child. The main thing to remember, though, is not to give up. Unless you persevere and stay in contact, your young child will easily learn to live without you and will forget who you are. Although your job is a difficult one, it is not impossible and it *is* worthwhile. No one else is as important to a child as her two parents.

Much of what you as a long-distance parent can do with a young child depends on the cooperation of your ex-partner. Your relationship with your ex-partner is a critical element in maintaining contact with a young child. This will be discussed in greater detail in Chapter 4, "Your Relationship with Your Ex-Partner."

Your child is four years old or younger. What can

you do to be an involved parent across the miles? How can you be a presence in your child's life even though you live two thousand miles away?

Stories

A wonderful way to be with your child every day is to record yourself reading bedtime stories to your child. This will involve having a tape recorder at your home and a tape recorder at your child's home. The financial outlay is definitely worth the pleasure this will bring your child. The cooperation of your child's custodial parent is an essential ingredient to the success of this type of contact.

One local parent I know has come to depend on the bedtime stories her ex-partner has recorded on tape. As soon as her daughter is in her pajamas, this mother turns on the tape machine and her daughter gets right into bed to listen to her father's stories.

> His voice is such a calming influence on my daughter. When he gets to the end of a few pages, he always says, 'That's all for now. I'll read to you again tomorrow night. Goodnight, my sweet girl. I love you.' I don't know why it gets me teary but it does. Maybe it reminds me of my father reading to me when I was a little girl.—Maria

You won't have to spend most of your waking hours recording stories in order to meet the need for a nightly tale. Young children love repetition and will be glad to hear the same story over and over again. For some children, having the same book in front of them that you are reading from is an extra pleasure. Then they can turn pages and look at pictures as you read, with some guidance from the parent at home.

As soon as they are able, encourage your children to record their own stories on tape for you. Explain to your child that you will be able to hear his voice in the same way that he hears yours. He might sing you a song, or tell you about his day in nursery school. A supply of mailing envelopes, already addressed and stamped, will give your child a sense of independence as he puts the tape into the envelope and then into the mailbox, with a lift from a parent. This will also make it easier for the local parent to return the tapes to you.

Do you have the facilities to make a videotape? Does your child's local parent own a videocassette recorder? If so, you can make a video of yourself talking to your child, telling a story about yourself as a young child. You might sing a song for your child, one that you know your child already knows, or one that your grandmother sang to you. Accompany yourself on the piano or guitar, or even a simple xylophone or drum. You can play peek-a-boo on the video, hiding behind a chair and then reappearing. Walk around your house and take pictures. Go outside and film the street where you live. Be creative. Let your imagination go. Keep your child in mind at all times as you make the tape and your love will shine through.

Young children are very visually oriented. They enjoy looking at picture books and pointing to what's familiar. Make a photo album for your child and include pictures of yourself, your parents, and other family members. Include photos of the house or apartment you live in now, the rooms in your house or apartment, and the surrounding areas. Be sure to mark each picture with simple, clearly written descriptions. This photo album can be a book your child will enjoy for many years.

Alison, age nine, remembers a photo album her mom made for her when she was very young.

My mom didn't have enough money to keep me after my parents got divorced, so she moved back to her parents' house and I stayed with my dad. She made me a beautiful photo album with pictures of everyone in her family. I still treasure that book and I'm almost all grown now.

One long-distance father I know made two such photo albums. He sent one to his son and kept one at his house. When his son came to visit, they enjoyed looking at the photo album together, and they added to it with pictures from each visit.

Another visual project you can make for a young child is a story that is written with pictures from magazines that represent words. Instead of writing out the word "house," for instance, you would paste a picture of a house on the page. If you are artistic, you can draw pictures to represent words in the story. The more pictures, the better. Your story might look like this:

I love [picture of a heart] my new house [picture of a house]. It has two bed [picture of a bed] rooms, one [1] for you [a finger pointing out] and one [1] for me [finger pointing to oneself]. There are trees [picture of trees] and flowers [pictures here] all around. The train [picture of train] station is nearby. Most of all, I love [heart] you!

Keep it simple and your child will be proud of being able to "read" it all by himself.

Phone Calls

Call your child regularly, even though he is young and won't be able to carry on a lengthy conversation. Let him hear the sound of your voice, and listen to his voice. Talk about animals and ask your child to make the sound of various animals. Sing a song with him that you heard on *Sesame Street*. (As a long-distance parent, you do have to keep up on these things!) Ask your child to sing a song he learned in nursery school that day. Above all, tell your child how much you love him, what a wonderful little boy he is, and when you will talk or visit with each other again.

It is natural to feel discouraged if your child isn't particularly responsive on the phone. Do not expect much. Some children, even young ones, like to chatter on the telephone. Others have no interest in it at all, even if it is their father calling them. Be patient and keep calling.

Transitional Objects

I'm sure you have seen a young child clutching her favorite blanket or teddy bear. These transitional objects are used by young children to deal with their own separation anxiety. Elaine Radiss, M.S.S., a family therapist who teaches courses in child development, says that "before children develop object constancy, that is, before they can recall the parent in their own mind, they transfer their emotional attachment to an inanimate object. The child becomes very attached to a doll or stuffed animal and insists on going to bed with it, if not on dragging it around all day long."

As a long-distance parent, you can buy your child a special transitional object. Of course, what you pick out as special may not be what your child chooses. What parent doesn't recall his child clinging for dear life to a ratty old blanket when he had many beautiful stuffed animals in his room.

When your child comes to visit you, he may get attached to something at your home. It might be a pillow or a piece of clothing or a book. Send this object home with your child, with a suggestion to the child to connect the object to you. You can say to your child, "When you go home, you'll look at this and think of me and remember the good times we have together."

Irene told me about the time her young son returned from a visit with his father clutching a cloth book of nursery rhymes. She had a very difficult time separating him from that book.

He would not put that book down. He took it with him into the bathtub, he went to bed with it, he put it on the table next to his food. When I would try to get it away from him, he became a holy terror. Finally, I asked him what was so special about the book and he said it was from his daddy's house. I never tried to take it from him again. It was some powerful book!

Mail

Young children love getting mail, even if they can't read it themselves. It makes them feel very important. Send your child a picture that you drew or a postcard with a pretty picture on it. Send photos of yourself that your child can hang up in her room. Send a photo of the two of you taken together. Take a series of pictures in a photo booth—the kind that used to be four for a quarter and are now four for a dollar. Make funny faces, strike a humorous pose. Young kids love silliness.

Send some stamped, self-addressed envelopes to your child and explain what they are for. Tell your child to put a picture in it and send it to you. The local parent will need to cooperate with this: but the idea is to make it as simple as possible for your child to keep in touch with you.

Special Gifts

Send little gifts—the keyword here is little—that are appropriate to your child's age. Go to a toy store or a bookstore and enlist the aid of a knowledgeable salesperson. Describe your child, his age, and his interests as best you know them, and ask what a good *little* gift might be—perhaps a puzzle or a pop-up book.

An interesting idea for a puzzle is to take a picture of yourself and then have it blown up, say to eleven inches by fourteen inches. Then either glue it to a piece of heavy cardboard or have it mounted on a thin piece of wood. Then cut out pieces (using a jigsaw if mounted on wood), rather larger sections for a young child, that when put together form the picture of you. If you find your puzzle-making energies unleashed, make a puzzle from a picture of your child, then do one of the grandparents he usually does not get to see. The variations on puzzle-making are endless.

Other appropriate gifts for young children include some balloons, stickers they can use themselves, old clothes they can use for dressing up, markers for drawing. Use your imagination and remember to keep the gift small—and appropriate to the age of your child. (One of my favorite catalogs, filled with imaginative gifts for children, is called *Wireless,* from Minnesota Public Radio, 274 Fillmore Avenue East, St. Paul, MN 55107.)

Visits

The more visits you have with your young child, the more direct physical contact you have, and the easier it will be for you to form a strong connection. Younger children don't remember all that well and need a lot of reinforcement. The more often you talk with your child, hug her, play games with her, just be with her, the more you will become a part of her and she will remember you.

Arranging for visits with a very young child can be problematic. If your relationship with your child's other parent is relatively calm, it will be easier for you to see your child. You might be able to go to the local parent's home for several afternoon visits. If your relationship with your ex-partner is not a cooperative one, arrange to see your child at a grandparent's house. Take your child to nursery school one day and arrange to spend the morning there. Go to the zoo together or to a neighborhood park.

If you have acted irresponsibly in the past, you will probably have to prove yourself to the local parent in order to take the child to your home for an extended visit. If this is the case, go slowly. Prove yourself responsible in the local parent's territory first. Be where you say you'll be. Return the child when you say you will. Don't give the local parent any reason to deny your requests to see your child. Put your partial custody and visitation agreement in writing, and expect it to change as your child gets older.

If you don't live close enough to see your young child more than once or twice a year, or your financial resources are limited, you will have to concentrate on building and maintaining a connection with your child through the mail and by phone. You have a hard job ahead of you, one that will require a major commitment on your part. If you forget your child, your child will forget you. The younger the child, the more of an impact you need to make, so that the child will remember you and have you inside him. This requires contact—physical and emotional contact.

Five- to Ten-Year-Olds

Children who are old enough to go to school become exposed to a wide variety of experiences and adventures that you, as a long-distance parent, should be aware of. They become more conscious of the world around them, they learn to read and write, they become more social. They are able to take more responsibility for themselves and their lives. Their interests develop by leaps and bounds. All this is grist for the long-distance mill. You can use your child's developing sense of himself to your advantage as you continue to nurture your long-distance relationship.

Five- to ten-year-olds go out into the world. They take in more information about what family life is like. They visit at friends' homes and observe their families. They are influenced by people other than their parents. Their teachers, the crossing guard, the scout leader, all become important people in your child's life. There is a lessening of the idealization of children's own families as they become aware of other families.

Whereas younger children should be loved unconditionally by their parents, school-age children want to be noticed and praised for their accomplishments—the things they do. They have to start performing and work for the approval of their parents. They want to be recognized for their efforts.

If you're a long-distance parent of a school-age child, you need to be as aware of the child's daily life as possible, so that you know what to notice, what to praise, and what to approve of.

Your Child at School

Write to your child's school, introduce yourself, and request that information be sent to you concerning schedules, test results, grades, and specific events. Tell your child that you have done this. The school will write back to you if there is any problem sending you this information. You are entitled to this information if you have joint custody or are the child's legal parent without physical custody. School personnel must be very careful about who they release information to, so you may be asked to supply legal documents regarding your status in the child's life.

There is a federal law, FERPA (Family Educational Rights and Privacy Act), which delineates thirty-two rights that a noncustodial parent has. Each state has endorsed either all thirty-two rights or portions of the act. All states, however, have agreed to the portion that gives the noncustodial parent the right to see grades and other records from school pertaining to the child. This includes all public schools as well as any private or church-related school if the school takes one cent or more in federal funds. This essentially means all schools.

The FERPA office in Washington, D.C. (Room 4512, Switzer Building, Department of Education, Washington, D.C. 20202), has been maintained since 1974 for the benefit of assisting noncustodial parents in obtaining cooperation from their child's school. Ken Lewis, Ph.D., director of the Child Custody Evaluation Services of Philadelphia, encourages noncustodial parents to find out about FERPA. Dr. Lewis says, "In all aspects of the divorced child's two lives—two homes, two churches, two sets of friends—one place where there tends to be neutrality is the school. FERPA is an action-based program which requires the school to become active between the child and the long-distance parent."

As a long-distance parent, you can join your child's parent-child-teacher association. You can and should visit your child's classroom during the school day (with proper notification given to school authorities). The next time you are visiting your child in her home surroundings, schedule an appointment with your child's teacher and/ or principal so that you are more aware of a very important part of your child's life. School personnel will also be aware of your interest in your child and will be able to call on you (suggest they call you collect) if your assistance is ever needed. Tell your child and your ex-partner that you are planning to do this and explain your intentions.

Ask your child to save all kinds of school work for you—reports, test papers, essays, anything and everything. Supply your child (or the local parent) with stamps and self-addressed envelopes and let your child know that you are genuinely interested in her work. Howard loved to draw and was very pleased to see his daughter develop an interest in art. He gave his daughter big envelopes and lots of different denominations of stamps so she could mail the drawings she did at school to him.

I hung them up all over my house, so when she came to visit, she could see how proud I was of her work, and that I had it displayed all over.

Remember, children of this age want to be praised for the work they do and want to be noticed for the effort they put forth. So put forth effort of your own and let your child know how you feel about her work. Howard began to tell his daughter what he especially liked about her drawings. He made mention of her use of color, of the variety in her subject matter. He noticed her sense of space and balance. Howard's long-distance interest in his daughter's artwork enhanced her own enthusiasm for art, and she loved his appreciation of her work.

Were you proud of your son because of a book report he did? Read that book yourself and discuss it with your son over the phone. The more you put yourself into your child's daily life, the more you will have to talk about over the phone, and the more intelligent questions you will be able to ask. If you go out of your way to find and read a book your son has just read, he'll have to know that you really care about him.

We live in the age of computers, and many schools and businesses are equipped with fairly advanced models. Most children are quite adept at using computers and can teach you what you need to know to keep up with them. Can you do graphics on your computers? Write electronic mail, E-mail, if your computers are equipped with modems at each end. If you have an account with MCIMail, one person deposits a letter and the other checks to see if there's mail for them. Using a word processor makes the task much easier for a parent who doesn't like to write.

Use your child's developing interests to expand your own, and see if you can get your child excited about your own special interests. Together you can have a meaningful long-distance relationship. Let your child know that you want a full report of her participation in various events—sports, plays, musical events, dance recitals, schoolwork. And then be sure to respond appropriately.

Watching TV

Watch television together. Find out what your child's favorite TV shows are and plan to spend the evening together, checking in by phone before the show begins, once at the mid-show commercial, and then again at the end to discuss the show. You might want to save this way of being together for a Saturday or Sunday morning, when the long-distance phone rates are least expensive. Be prepared, then, for some cartoon shows! In any case, you can keep the calls short and you can share some special time together.

Using the Mail

Remember the old song from the TV show *Name That Tune?* Letters, we get letters, we get stacks and stacks of letters! *Use the mail.* When children of this age begin to learn to read and write, letters are a wonderful way of bonding. You can use letters to tell about your daily life, about your ideas about life. You can clip out an article or a picture from the newspaper that relates to your child. You can send a cartoon that reminds you of your son. Your letters can be a source of encouragement to your child. "I'll be rooting for you when you play your soccer game this weekend."

Write to your child about how you felt when you were his age. What memories do you have of your first day at school? Tell about a particular teacher you had who influenced you in some way. Is your daughter having trouble with her best friend? Write about your first fight with your best friend when you were her age. Children love to know about your childhood, so tell them! Did you take music lessons when you were young? Write about what that was like for you and how your own mother would yell at you to practice. Were you in the school plays? Write about how excited and how scared you were just before the performance began. Relate what experiences your child is now having to experiences you had as a child.

Cindy, age twelve, talks about the wonderful letters she gets from her long-distance dad and how much they mean to her. When she gets a letter, she goes into her room, closes the door, and makes believe she is actually spending the next period of time with her dad. What Cindy likes best about her dad's letter is that he always writes about himself.

He doesn't hide his feelings from me. He tells me when he's sad about something and when he's angry about something. And he also always writes something about something I've written to him about. There's a lot of back and forth in our letters. He saves mine and I save his. We joke about publishing our letters in a book one day.

What do you do when your child doesn't write back to you? How can you encourage your child to write? A long-distance father described his policy to me, knowing that he might be accused of bribery.

My kid loves money. He'll do anything to earn an extra fifty cents. A dollar bill is big bucks for him. Our deal is that when I get a letter from him, and I mean a real letter, not a scribble of "How are you? I'm fine. Love, Matthew," I send him fifty cents in my next letter to him. I get letters regularly now and I love getting them and I don't care if I'm bribing him. I've learned a lot about him through our letters and they mean a lot to me.—William

Children like the autonomy of being able to mail their letters to you themselves. Make it easier for your children to write to you by supplying them with stacks of stamped, self-addressed envelopes. Send them colorful stationery appropriate to their interests. Look for music designs, sports motifs, or airplanes and trains.

Use the mail to send special treats. Every once in a while, include a dollar bill in your letter. Enclose a stick of chewing gum. Send a funny drawing you made. You don't have to be an artist to amuse a child.

Send a packet of seeds that your child can plant in the spring; you can both look forward to having him tell you all about the planting and blossoming as the weather gets warmer. Send picture postcards of all the places you visit, as well as postcards of the place you are living in now. When your child comes to visit you, you can show him all the sights he saw on the picture postcards. Fred, a long-distance father for five years, travels a lot for his job. He makes it a point to carry postcard stamps with him so that as soon as he buys the postcard, he can write it, stamp it, and send it off immediately. "I always mail separate ones to each of my kids," says Fred. "I don't lump them together in my mind, so I don't lump them together when I write to them. My postcards are tacked up all over their bedroom walls, so I figure I'm with them all the time."

Use the mail to send riddles to your child and ask her to write the answers back to you. You can get an endless supply of riddles and jokes (which you can use in phone calls as well) from children's books at the library. Take out a few books and photocopy pages of riddles to use in subsequent letters.

If you are not a writer, if you have writer's block, if you do not feel especially creative, or if you find yourself forgetting to write to your child, a useful kit has been developed to help stimulate correspondence between parents and children. *The Written Connection* provides stationery, mailers for the child to respond to you, projects appropriate for each month, calendars to fill in, stickers, and helpful hints about writing to your long-distance child. While it is fairly expensive, $49.95, it does provide a written system of communicating that can be used each week during the year. For more information, call or write Expressions Unlimited, Inc., 33 E. Comstock, Suite 4, Chandler, AZ 85224 (1-800-334-3143). Be sure to specify the age of your child when ordering.

The Preadolescent: Eleven to Thirteen

Preadolescent children are becoming more aware of their own sexual identity. They closely watch the changes taking place in their own bodies. They may not particularly like members of the opposite sex, but they become very conscious themselves of being either boys or girls.

They might start to use dirty words. They get sloppy and don't rush into the shower. Eleven- to thirteen-year-olds are very involved with their own friends and their own activities.

This is a time when the same-sex parent and opposite-sex parent can take on special functions. As the same-sex parent, you should make lots of opportunities to talk with your children about their awakening interest in their own sexuality and gender identity. This is a time to talk with your children about newly developing interests in the opposite sex or problems they might be having in that arena. You become a model to your children of how to be a man or woman in the world. A father teaches his son about respecting females; a woman teaches her daughter about having consideration for men.

Opposite-sex parents teach their children, through their own behavior, to appreciate and value the sex they are. A father prizes his daughter, values her, acknowledges her for her accomplishments and her appearance. A father adores his daughter, and by doing so, helps her feel good about herself as a female. Physical, nonsexual contact with a daughter helps her to be physically familiar with males. All along, the way the father behaves with his daughter lets her know she can have it all: she can be an architect, or a neurosurgeon, and a wife and mother, if that's what she chooses.

Carrie, a woman in her early twenties who had a long-distance relationship with her dad for most of her childhood years, remembers a picture her father took of her on one of their visits together. He sent it to her and wrote on the back that she was his "beautiful, growing-up girl." Carrie kept that picture in her wallet for years. "It just made me feel so good whenever I read what he wrote." A long-distance father can use every opportunity to tell his daughter how wonderful she is, how lovely she looks, and how proud he is to have her as his daughter.

Long-distance mothers, too, have a special role to play with their sons. At a time when a boy is learning about his own sexuality and his friends might be teasing

him because the girls like him, his mother can be nurturing and reassuring to her son. She need not be the
disciplinarian if his father is there to do that. She can be
the parent who loves her son unconditionally, who tells
him how handsome he looks, what a strong boy he is,
and what a fine man he will grow up to be. The boy
experiences his mother as strong, competent, and loving,
and this lays the groundwork for what he will look for in
women when he is ready to choose a mate.

Roberta, a long-distance mother for the past four
years, says that she makes it a point to tell her son in
every phone call, in every letter, about ten times during
every visit, how wonderful she thinks he is.

> He doesn't seem to get tired of hearing how much I
> love him and how proud I am of him. I know that
> some woman will be very lucky indeed to have such
> a fine husband as my son. Do I sound like I'm brag-
> ging? I guess I am.

Whether a same-sex or opposite-sex parent, the long-
distance parent of an eleven- to thirteen-year-old has a
lot to work with. Tapping into the child's particular interests and finding ways to relate to his life is the special
task at hand. If your child is a sports enthusiast, there
are lots of ways to share this interest across the miles.
George Newman, in his book *101 Ways to Be a Long-
Distance Super-Dad*, describes predicting with your
youngster who will win important sporting events
throughout the year. Friendly competition develops between parent and child, which lends itself to endless discussion in letters, phone calls, and of course, in watching
the events themselves on TV.

Joseph always encouraged his daughter's interest in
sports. She seemed to be a natural athlete, good at soccer
and softball. He says:

> Now, much to my great joy, she's learning how to play
> tennis. When important games and matches are on

TV, we always have a date to watch them together. Sometimes we bet a dollar on who will win, which adds to her excitement. Mostly, I'm just so pleased that she shares my interest in sports and that we have a lot to talk about together.

A long-distance father can thrill his young daughter by sending her a corsage on the eve of an important debut. A long-distance mother can acknowledge her son for a job well done by sending a certificate of excellence, written in calligraphy. Whatever you do, remember to praise your children and praise them again, for their efforts, and for just being themselves. You will be rewarded with a loving long-distance relationship.

Ages Fourteen to Eighteen

These young people are full of questions about you and your life and are full of opinions as to what is right and wrong. They want to know about the real meaning of divorce, about why your marriage broke up, about why you left town. They might be full of recriminations, blaming one parent or another, accusing you of abandoning the family when things got rough. They will force you to rehash old history and make you think about things you'd rather forget.

At this point, you have to figure out how much is appropriate to reveal when very pointed questions are asked. For instance, you might be questioned about an affair you had many years ago that your child has just become aware of. You do not have to tell all; you can say you do not care to discuss these matters and that they are not your child's concern. But know that this will not satisfy your adolescent, who is now a person to be reckoned with and cannot be dismissed easily. What and how you tell your child depends on your relationship, how comfortable you feel talking about these things, and how able your child is to hear the truth. You may want to postpone being interrogated about the details, but you can talk about how you felt at the time and what your marriage was like.

The scrutiny of your romantic life may go on, however, to include your present relationships. An inquisitive adolescent will want to know about your current love life, as well. The same rules apply to determine your response. You may be fairly comfortable in divulging information about your sex life. Most parents are not. You are not necessarily an uptight, secretive parent if you choose to keep this information private. Think about your child, how you think he will react, and how he will use the knowledge you give him.

Children of divorce, and long-distance children in particular, are especially sensitive to feeling abandoned. A new romantic involvement for you can feel very threatening for them. Your children want and need reassurance that they are still number one in your heart and that whatever new relationship you may form in the future, you will not neglect them or forget them. In discussing delicate subjects with your long-distance child, consider first what will strengthen that relationship. Above all, do not dismiss your child's questions as unimportant. You want your child to feel that she can come to you with difficult, uncomfortable questions and that you will listen well and respond as best you can.

Some long-distance parents find that their relationships with their teenage children shift. Adolescents are much more concerned about their social life, which centers at school and in their neighborhood. They start making their own plans and want less to do with their parents. Do you give your children a choice about where they spend their free time? Do you insist that they come visit you over the summer as they have always done, or do you recognize some new developing interests of theirs and allow them to go on a special trip with friends?

I've been flying out to California to visit my dad three times a year for the past thirteen years—all summer, and for Christmas and Easter vacations. I've never been on a vacation with friends. I've never gone to summer camp with my local friends. I've never gone on a teen tour or anything like that. I don't question that and neither do my parents. It's just part of my life.—Elana, age seventeen

Some teenagers, though, resent the long-distance visits and wish they could eliminate some of them in favor of their social life at home. Perhaps there are some compromises you can make. Consider a visit to your child in her local surroundings.

The first time my son Josh told me he was going to be in a musical at school, I was absolutely thrilled. I had always shared my interest in music with him, and although I knew he liked music and had talent in that area, he never extended himself to participate in any musical activities. There was no question in my mind that I would go to Vermont to see his performance. I could barely contain myself when he came on stage. "That's my son!" I wanted to yell out. "Isn't he great?" He *was* great, but of course I wouldn't want to embarrass him by being an obnoxious, if proud, mother—a long-distance one at that.

Over the long-distance years, Josh has been in many musical productions at school and I have attended every one. It's a strong link we have together and I want to reinforce it in every way I can, showing him by my presence how much it means to me. During one particular performance, I was struck with how little I knew of Josh's everyday life. I knew some of his friends, but none of their parents, who were also at the performance. I felt very isolated, like a foreigner in a strange land.

Other long-distance parents have shared similar experiences. Visiting a child in his home territory is a poignant time. You become much more aware of all you are missing. You notice friends coming and going, you get caught up firsthand in their enthusiasm for a school or sports event. You see typical adolescent behavior—

languishing for hours, or imitating rock stars. Those are experiences of being a parent that are often denied to you long-distance. Being there, being in a child's home surroundings gives you a very different experience of your own child. It can be a very sad, touching time for a long-distance parent, yet rewarding in its own way.

On my visits, I concentrated on how wonderful Josh looked on stage—a lot of presence, very handsome; his personality came forth and his singing was great. The day after one show Josh was in a choral performance and received an award for being named to sing in the All-New England Chorus. I was teary throughout the concert, listening to him sing parts of the Mozart "Requiem" as I had in high school, and remembering his performance the night before. I also thought about him teaching himself to play the guitar, as I once did, and of his enthusiasm for rock 'n' roll. There was no question that I had passed on my love of music and the joy of expressing oneself through music to him. I am a strong part of him in that way, and I know he has carried on a strong musical tradition in my family.

What interests have *you* developed with your child that can be intensified during her teenage years? Did you share an interest in geography with your youngster that can be continued now through planning a very special trip together? Can you create an art project together? Again, it is up to you to tap into your child's interests and make that part of your relationship.

Be warned, though. Part of being an adolescent means being rebellious. An eight-year-old child is not given any choice about visiting you, but a teenager's wishes must be taken into account. Some adolescents may feel too hurt and angry to visit, or they may make it very difficult for you to be involved with them.

If your relationship with your child was not a high priority for you over the years, he would have felt it. Now that you want more closeness, your teenager may want more distance. Your teenager may be experiencing the pain and loss of the original separation all over again and may not want to spend time with you. The local parent may even be encouraging the teenager to stay home or may, in some way, be sabotaging your relationship with your child.

You need to talk to your child to find out what is going on. Ask your child to tell you her feelings about coming to visit you—all of them. And then be prepared to listen without being defensive. Investigate whether the local parent is influencing this decision. You can encourage your adolescent to spend time with you, but you cannot force her to. Keep saying what you want your relationship to be, but you must go slowly and be prepared to withdraw for a time. Increasing pressure on an angry adolescent is not the best technique to achieve your goal. It is very painful for a parent to be rejected by a child, but equally painful for the child to feel rejected by the parent, whether the rejection is real or imagined. So you must do everything you can to stay in communication with your child, even if it seems not appreciated at the time.

Visits, Again

Visits have only been mentioned in passing, but of course they are an essential way of keeping in touch with your long-distance child. The extent and duration of the visits you have with your child depend on many factors— your financial resources, the age of your child, the priority you place on visits, and, once again, on the co-operation and relationship you have with your ex-partner.

The younger your child, the more important visits are: They give your child direct contact with you so the memory of you stays with him. Visits, planning for them, the expectations they bring, and then the sadness at the leave-taking make them dramatic experiences for the long-distance parent and child. The drama gets repeated over and over again, and in time, people learn to cope with this upheaval in their lives (see Chapter 6, "Reunions and Good-byes."

Visiting can be a stressful time, as well as a joyous one. Everyone is filled with fantasies about what the visit will be like. Both long-distance parent and child will anticipate the visit eagerly, with high hopes of an intimate, wonderful time together. It doesn't always work out that way, however. Some visits are filled with the unexpected, and both parent and child may feel disappointed, let down, and hurt that things didn't go as planned.

Instead of allowing the time together to be ruined, use the experience to reassure your child that all is not lost. You are still together; even though things didn't go as planned, you can make the best of the time you have left. Life is full of rocky events, and although it might not be fair for long-distance parents and children to experience those in the short time they are together, we don't always get to choose when things will happen to us. If you can talk with your child about what is going on, and share the uncomfortable feelings you may have, you will have a memorable visit, even one you might laugh about later on. A sign I had on my refrigerator for many years said, "If it'll be funny later, it's funny now." Pass it on. Being flexible is a key ingredient in having successful visits. There is a lot of unpredictability when people come together after long absences.

You and your long-distance child can have fun planning visits before they happen. What would you like to do together? If you are planning something special, do the planning together, in letters and phone calls. Are you going on a little trip? Get maps of the areas you'll visit and send them to your child with the route clearly outlined.

Many long-distance parents have found that they used to fill the visits with their child with a fast-paced, frantic activity, just for the sake of keeping busy. There is a temptation to allay any strain in an awkward relationship. There is also a temptation to buy a visiting child's love with an endless stream of treats and gifts. With time,

however, those long-distance parents have learned that
the merry-go-round of activities in a short period of time
doesn't allow for the intimate times they and their children really prefer. Parents and their children feel less
exhausted and overloaded after a visit when they have
shared some calm, quiet moments together, the kind that
make for long-lasting, meaningful memories.

My son and I enjoy being together at home, listening
to music and making new tapes. We've made tapes of
different music for each other since Josh was very young,
and we have continued to do this throughout our separation. Josh will make me a tape of his favorite new music, so I don't get to be an old-fashioned, uncool parent.
For his birthday one year, I made him a tape that I called
Joshua Then and Now, after the movie of the same name.
I included all the songs he's enjoyed over the years, from
nursery rhymes to favorite folks songs, to camp songs
and then on to treasured rock 'n' roll tunes. So when he
comes to visit, our tradition of making tapes together
continues and we make copies for each of us to have.
The memories linger on.

Since Josh got out of the "I won't try anything on"
phase we have enjoyed shopping together. We go to South
Street in Philadelphia—"the hippest street in town"—
which is startlingly different from any street in Burlington, Vermont. What amazes me is seeing Josh's changing
sense of style. Since I don't see him for long periods of
time, it seems that a formerly fairly conservative dresser
has turned into a fairly flashy dresser before my very
eyes. He now likes New Wave clothes, funky styles. As
a long-distance parent, I don't see gradual changes in his
taste, but only see the great leaps forward he has taken
since his last visit. I swallow hard and say, "Those shoes?
Really?" Quickly, I answer myself, "Sure! Why not?"
I am proud of his nice sense of color and style and that
he chooses clothes wisely, considering finances as well
as looks. An extra added attraction to our shopping trips
is seeing Josh out in the world, dealing charmingly with
sales people, interacting with people we meet on the

street—things a long-distance parent usually doesn't get to see.

Plan something new that *you* can do on your next visit with your child that will make for a fond memory later on. That's what you want to do: make your visits long-lasting in your minds.

Isolina Ricci, in her book *Mom's House, Dad's House,* describes a special "thinking box" that a parent collects in between visits "that shows where your heart is. Extra postcards bought on a trip, . . . a small piece of driftwood, . . . an idea you had, dated with time and place, put in a special box or container, awaiting the child's presence." When the child is visiting with you, you can pore over it together, telling stories about each item in the thinking box, adding physical proof for your child about how much he is a part of your everyday life.

Little things mean a lot to children; visits need not be filled with extravaganzas in order for them to be memorable for kids. Yes, trips are fun, but what children really want when they visit is an experience of you. They want you to give of yourself to them, and that is what they will take home with them. The quiet talks, the walks on the beach collecting seashells the child can take home, the meal you cooked together—those events can be truly memorable.

The longer the visits can be, the more bonding can take place. A child who stays with his other parent for two weeks at Christmas and Easter and for six to eight weeks during the summer can develop a strong relationship with that parent. Ordinary events of life will happen—illness and cranky times as well as pleasant times. Parent and child will have an opportunity to develop their own patterns of relating together in good times and bad.

Make sure your child knows when you will see each other again. Give her a calendar so she can mark down the special dates. Whether you are discussing the next visit or the next phone call, continuity is important in maintaining and strengthening your long-distance relationship. You can't afford to forget a birthday or a holiday. Make each contact as special as you can—an extra phone call, a humorous card, a little gift in the mail. Your child hasn't forgotten you and wants to know that you are thinking of her, that she is a high priority in your life, and that you are willing to do whatever it takes to have a close relationship with her.

CHAPTER 4

Your Relationship with Your Ex-Partner

The greatest fear that a long-distance parent has is that he will be shut out of his child's life forever, that his ex-partner will cut off all communication to his child, especially if the child is young. Letters won't be delivered, arrangements for planned visits won't be honored, and, in effect, his relationship with his child will be severed. This scenario is infrequent, but it does happen. In some instances, a parent is determined to destroy the bond between long-distance parent and child and does so in a willful, malicious way. This parent will rip up letters before the child sees them, will even go so far as to lie to the child about phone calls received. ''Your father didn't even remember to call you on your birthday,'' a mother says to a heartbroken little boy, when, in fact, the father did call.

This extremely destructive behavior is uncommon, but the fantasy of this occurring strikes fear into the heart of every long-distance parent. A long-distance parent has to trust that the local parent will honor the relationship he has with his child, that the local parent will if not promote the relationship at least be neutral about it. Later in this chapter I will discuss what to do if you cannot trust your ex-mate to support your relationship with your child and what to do if your situation is that uncommon one where you are actively prevented from having a long-distance relationship with your child.

Dr. Marla Isaacs, former director of the Families of

Divorce Project at the Philadelphia Child Guidance Clinic and coauthor of *The Difficult Divorce,* divides relationships in postdivorce couples into three categories: friendly, neutral, and hostile.

Friendly parents are those who can cooperate easily regarding the needs of their children. These parents value the relationship they each have with the child and do everything they can to promote that relationship. They can talk on the phone without getting into fights. They might plan to celebrate an important event in the child's life together, such as a birthday or graduation from high school. If a problem arises with the child, friendly parents use each other to solve the problem and work out an appropriate course of action.

> I have a very close relationship with my ex-husband. We are still very fond of each other and even though he has remarried, we talk on the phone during the week. My son lives with him, and the closeness I feel with my ex-husband makes it a whole lot easier for me to be so far away from my son.—Cecilia

Cooperative, warm feelings characterize those ex-partners who are on friendly terms. While they may not talk on the phone every week, friendly parents are those who communicate fairly easily with one another and want to cooperate with each other. Later on in this chapter, I will discuss variations in friendly relationships between ex-partners.

A neutral relationship between ex-partners is characterized by parents who, while they may not like each other, have managed to put aside their bitterness for the sake of the best interests of the child. These parents talk to each other to take care of business, to make arrangements for visits, and perhaps will call each other in an emergency. Neutral parents don't do anything to help or hinder the relationship between them and the child.

> I never say anything negative to my daughter about her father. I don't say anything positive either, be-

cause I don't feel positive. I just try not to get in the way of their relationship and that works out best for my daughter.—Helen

Do you as a long-distance parent want to be called in times of difficulty or crisis? Tell the local parent how you want to be involved. Do you want to know if your child got into a fight at school, or is running a high fever? You might wonder what you can do about either of these events from a distance. The first thing you can do is to offer support to the local parent. If you can be a source of comfort to your ex-partner in these times, or can offer clear thinking during a discussion of the problem, you are doing a great deal not only for your child, but to further cooperation between you and your ex-partner.

A hostile relationship is one where anger and bitterness mark almost every interaction. There is little trust or cooperation between parents, and it is very difficult for the long-distance parent to have a relatively calm relationship with his child. As one of my clients says,

I can count on my ex-wife for one thing—to make my life miserable. This was true when I lived around the corner from her and it's true now that I live fifteen hundred miles away. She makes it virtually impossible for me to continue being the kind of father I want to be.—Bruce

Bruce does have some options in this situation. He could give up and hope to reunite with his children when they go away to college and have some autonomy; he could battle it out, phone call by phone call, in the hopes of maintaining contact with his kids; or he could just plod on and have minimal contact with his ex-wife. His children will get older, and he will eventually be able to deal with them directly, making his plans directly with them.

Bruce has done everything. He has involved his ex-wife's parents, in the hopes of having them convince her that she is being destructive to her children by keeping him away from them. He has written letters to the children explaining how he feels. He is not always sure they receive them. He has stayed in touch with his children's teachers so he knows how they're doing in school. Sometimes he doesn't call at all for a while because he is not feeling strong enough to withstand his ex-wife's animosity.

Since Bruce has been in therapy with me, he has committed himself again to reaching out to his children, working out whatever arrangements he can to speak with them on the phone and to see them whenever possible. If his ex-wife is hostile to him, he keeps his purpose in mind, tries not to get into an argument, and stays focused on what he was calling about. "I'd like to speak to my daughter, please," he repeats over and over again. Now that his children are getting a bit older, Bruce can arrange for them to call him collect from a pay phone, or from a friend's house. This might seem sneaky, but it has saved Bruce and his children a lot of aggravation. Recently, Bruce's wife has diminished her attacks on him, probably because he is not as affected by them as he has been in the past. He no longer allows her to control his contacts with his children and has managed, through his perseverance and dedication, to arrange for a lengthy visit with his children this summer.

If you are embroiled in a hostile relationship with your ex-mate and are having great difficulty maintaining a relationship with your children, I strongly suggest that you seek outside help. You will naturally have many moments of uncertainty and feel impotent in the face of an antagonistic ex-mate. You need someone in your corner, someone who will help you sort out what's going on, listen to your feelings, and help you plot out your course of action. That person could be a friend, a relative, a counselor, a support group. Going it alone is unproductive.

What kind of relationship did you have with your ex-partner before you moved away? Were you friendly, neutral, or hostile? Most long-distance parents were not long-distance after the initial separation or divorce, but became so after several years of living near their ex-partner and child. Many had established a pattern of seeing their children on a regular basis, having phone contact regularly, and talking with their ex-mate from time to time about the children's needs.

The pattern that you established with your ex-mate of taking responsibility for your children prior to moving away will play a large part in how things are handled later on. If you have continued to be an active parent to your child while at the same time separating from your ex-mate emotionally, you will be in a better position to maintain a strong parenting position with your children. This does not automatically mean, however, that if you were minimally involved with your children during the marriage and the subsequent divorce period, that you will have minimal involvement with your children later on. Many parents, fathers in particular, have become acutely aware of the importance of their relationship with their children after a divorce takes place; they have rearranged their priorities and their lives so that they could spend more time with their children.

Whatever kind of relationship you established with your ex-partner and with your children while living in the same community, the geographical distance between you will create change. Many local parents feel a mixture of relief, anxiety at being abandoned, and general fear when the other parent moves away. The local parent is now left with the responsibilities for child-rearing and will probably not have any time off, except for long stretches at a time when your children visit their long-distance parent. Local parents also worry that their children will not be returned to them at the end of a visit. As Paul Simon sings, "Paranoia runs deep in the heartland."

Norma, whose two children used to visit their father every other weekend, remembers how she and her new husband came to cherish that child-free time together. Her ex-husband has since moved to California, and there are no more child-free weekends. Instead, there are child-free weeks at a time during the summer and Christmas vacations when her kids go to the West Coast to see their dad.

> It's been quite a change for all of us. No free weekends has been quite a hardship for us. On the flip side, this was my first Christmas without my boys and my husband and I had a blast! I didn't think I would survive without them for that long a time, but I did just fine.—Norma

Norma reports that her sons' father was not very responsible about keeping his word when he did live nearby. He disappointed his sons often by not showing up when he said he would. It was hit or miss for years. Norma covered up for her ex-husband, never saying anything bad about him to her boys, wanting to protect them from the hurt for as long as she could. It was only after she remarried that her ex-husband, worried that he'd lose his status as a father, began to take his parenting responsibilities more seriously.

Throughout this time, Norma remained on friendly terms with her ex-husband. She describes him as a "wonderful, sweet-hearted scatterbrain." She did nothing to alienate him from his sons and accommodated him wherever she could. Her first reaction to the news that her ex-husband was moving to California was one of panic. "I could see losing my babies, see them going to college there, meeting someone, and staying there to live." As time has gone on, Norma feels now that she would have a life of her own even if her children left home. Her relationship with her ex-husband and his second wife has remained friendly and Norma believes that her sons have benefited from the way she has handled her relationship with their father.

My own relationship with my ex-husband has been

a friendly one during the fourteen years of our post-divorce life. For the first ten years after our divorce, Jeff and I lived close to each other and had a fifty-fifty shared parenting arrangement for our son Josh. We spoke to each other on the phone fairly frequently about our son's needs and remained in the same social network, so that we saw each other frequently as well. During our marriage we had been good friends to each other, and this remained so after our divorce (well, after the first few angry years passed). There was no question that we could consult each other when problems arose concerning Josh. I don't think either of us ever considered any other way of being parents to Josh. He was our son and we both cared for him fully.

Since Jeff moved to Vermont and Josh moved with him, our relationship has remained friendly, although a bit more distant now. Initially, we spoke on the phone regularly, several times a week. Again, we consulted on difficulties and shared in the successes Josh was having in his new surroundings. We brainstormed together on how to solve various problems and I was always included in any major decision-making concerning Josh. The strong co-parenting arrangement we had living in the same community was transferred and adapted to long-distance co-parenting.

I have no doubt about the positive effects of our relationship on Josh. He knows that an end to a marriage does not necessarily mean an end to relationships. Co-operation is still possible. He sees his parents continue to be parents to him, first after a divorce living near each other and now living four hundred miles apart. Anything is possible in relationships!

What is your long-distance relationship like with your ex-partner? What would you like to change? Sit down with a piece of paper and make a list for yourself of the positive and negative aspects of your relationship with your ex-mate. There are several books available which include a series of checklists to help you evaluate your relationship with your ex-partner. Two such books are

Sharing the Children, by Robert E. Adler, Ph.D., and *Mom's House, Dad's House,* by Isolina Ricci. Issues such as communication, style of parenting, how you handle finances, and how you do business with each other are discussed. These checklists do not relate to long-distance parents per se, but can be helpful to you as a guide.

Long-distance parents who have their visitation and partial custody agreement in written form find that there is less room for misunderstandings concerning the long-distance parent's involvement with his child. A court order as to what the boundaries of partial custody will be should be kept clear and succinct. "Father will have children for four weeks during the summer, Christmas and Easter vacations, and will pay for transportation to his home. He will speak with the children on the phone at least two times a week." This agreement can always be changed, but it should be initially documented.

"[Even] if the relationship a divorced couple has is fairly amicable and one parent plans to move, I still recommend this agreement be written down," says Lynne Z. Gold-Bikin, a prominent family-law attorney. "The agreement can then be put in the safe deposit box, along with other insurance policies." When new pressures enter the family situation and one parent wants a modification of the agreement, the agreement can be the starting point for discussion.

Geographical distance creates change in postdivorce relationships. Some long-distance parents have learned, through some unhappy experiences, that they can no longer assume they have free and easy access to their child. Circumstances change, and so does the need to make more concrete arrangements. If your ex-wife has remarried, she may be less flexible and less willing to have you appear without much notice. She may not want you staying for a cup of coffee when you come to pick up your child, the way you used to. The geographical distance will probably put more emotional distance in your relationship with your ex-partner. As a result, you may need to make more formal arrangements to see your children and to be in touch with them regularly.

Some long-distance parents I've spoken with contend that the way they have learned to keep their relationship with their ex-partner trouble-free is to do what is expected of them, period.

> I send my support checks on time, I make myself available to my ex-wife in whatever way I can, I show up when I say I'll show up, I never miss a birthday or a holiday and I never bad-mouth her in front of the kids.—Doug

What can you do to create a neutral or friendly relationship with your ex-partner, so that you can have an open, uncluttered relationship with your child? As a long-distance parent who is in a vulnerable position in relation to your children, it is up to you not to do anything that would upset the local parent. The local parent can control your relationship with your children, so it would be stupid of you to do anything that would incur the wrath of that parent. Does that mean you have to walk around on tenterhooks, walking on eggs? Not exactly, but it *does* mean you have to be in control of yourself and your feelings and not blow off steam at your ex-mate just because you feel like it. You might have to hold your tongue in an argument, instead of saying something that would only lead to more distance and anger. You might want to tell the local parent how much you appreciate the good parenting she is doing on behalf of your children. (That would be a good idea no matter what your relationship is like! Everyone likes to know that their good efforts are being noticed.)

Don't be nasty or meet nastiness with nastiness. If you become aware of the fact that your ex-mate is making snide remarks about you in front of your child, don't retaliate in kind. These remarks are not helpful and don't necessarily promote a healthy adjustment for the child. Moreover, these statements are often inconsequential, need not be taken seriously, and, if ignored by the long-distance parent, do not have to get in the way of having a good relationship with your child.

Keep your purpose in mind: you want to maintain a close relationship with your child. If you make nasty remarks in return, it will, no doubt, get back to the local parent. Doing anything to upset the local parent could easily work against your goal, so it's best to work on rising above the offensive behavior and not getting caught up in it.

What if the custodial parent decides to leave town with the children, either to return to a hometown after a divorce or to move with a new mate? This leaves the other parent feeling furious, angry at having been abandoned by his family and not given any say in the matter.

George came to see me for therapy to help him deal with his rage at his ex-wife for taking his son away. He describes her move as "devastating" to him; he says that on several occasions he was verbally abusive to his ex-wife over the phone, threatening that he'd kidnap their son. After these incidents, George would feel extremely guilty, very distraught over his interactions with his ex-wife, and most important, miserable because he was then prevented from talking with his son. George felt out of control. I encouraged him to vent his rage and fury at his ex-wife with me. He needed to be able to express his feelings in a setting where his relationship with his son would not be jeopardized. Getting angry with his ex-wife would only make the situation worse. As I listened to him, I empathized with his situation, at the same time asking him to control his abusive, threatening behavior. With my help, George wrote the following letter to his ex-wife:

Dear Liz,
    I'm not interested in continuing the hostility between us, because I am convinced it is only hurting our son. I've been a jerk. I promise to do everything

I can to ease things between us. I've let my anger get in the way of having a relationship with my son.

I have no plans to kidnap Eddie. I never did. I was so angry I didn't know what to do. The next time I call, it will be to talk to Eddie. I'd also like to make plans to see him soon. I hope you won't make it any harder for me than it is now.

George

Afterward, George began to feel much better about himself and his situation. Even though it was still unbearable for him to be away from his son, he saw that there were ways he could handle himself so that he didn't make it any worse. He began to focus on how he could strengthen his relationship with his son, who was six years old; he knew that was his primary objective. He scheduled a weekly phone call with his son and began to see Eddie at regular intervals.

What started for George as a nightmare began to abate. His hostile relationship with his ex-wife, while never becoming friendly, did resolve into a more neutral stance. He learned that it wasn't important for him to express his rage over and over again to his ex-wife. She really wasn't interested. The only effect that had was to keep him away from his son.

George would like to be even more involved in his son's life, know what's going on with him in school, be called on by his ex-wife for support and advice. George has let Liz know that he is available to her. Being an active parent for George means being in control with Liz. He can't upset or anger her and then expect her to call on him for help. George is learning how to deal with his feelings of sadness and rage at being away from his son, and he is learning how to be a strong, reliable, long-distance parent.

Perhaps your relationship with your ex-partner is unsatisfactory and this prevents you from having the relationship you want with your child. You may feel a lot of pain about this, yet do not want to go into therapy. There are things you can do for yourself.

Write a letter to your ex-partner, explaining everything that you're feeling. Don't hold back, but don't mail the letter. The purpose of writing it would be to express yourself fully, without fear of repercussions. Although you can't reasonably expect that anything will change in relation to your ex-mate, it can be a cathartic experience for you.

Use the people you are close to as resources. Talk to a friend or to your new partner in order to gain some objectivity. See if you can find out what you are doing to perpetuate the distance between you and your ex-mate, and thus between you and your child. What do you gain by remaining distant? You are probably very much aware of the costs to you, but what about the gains? You may not want the responsibility of being very involved with your child. Talking with your ex-mate may take you on an emotional roller-coaster ride; seeing your child and then having to say good-bye again may open old wounds that are still festering. Understandably, you might just as well want to avoid all that. Yet, your problem won't be solved if you keep blaming your ex-mate without investigating your role in the circumstances. Whether you are in therapy or not, you will have to take a long, hard look at your present situation, how you are feeling, what led you to this point in your life, and what alternatives are available to you to make some needed changes.

Sally describes her relationship with her ex-husband as "neutral, although *he* would say it was friendly." Sally's sixteen-year-old son lives with his father, 280 miles away. She finds her ex-husband hard to communicate with, and there are many times that she has to weigh the importance of bringing up certain issues. She is often told by her ex-husband that she is too involved and that she worries too much. "If I come on too strong," says Sally, "he tries to make me feel like something's wrong with me.'' Sally finds that she has to choose her issues and that even though she knows her ex-husband may resent her interference, she perseveres if she feels something is important.

> Timing is crucial. I have to figure out if he's going to be receptive, and go from there. I wanted my ex-husband to discuss birth control and safe sex with my son. He told me it was too embarrassing. I told him I didn't care if it was embarrassing and that it would be more embarrassing for our son if I did it. I told him that he was the boy's father and that's what fathers talked to their sons about.

Quite a few long-distance mothers talked about the difficulty they had with their ex-partners discussing sensitive issues with them. There were some topics that were off-limits, some areas of their child's life that their fathers did not want to discuss. Many of these mothers got the feeling that their ex-partners felt they were being intrusive or too controlling, even from a distance. Cecilia, a long-distance mother whose son lives four hundred miles away, reports that her ex-husband doesn't like it when she gets concerned about a bad report her son might get at school. "I thought he needed a reading teacher, and his father took offense at that. I guess he thought I was questioning his parenting." Later, Cecilia said that her ex-husband called her back and was more open to the idea.

Some local parents feel threatened by advice and helpful hints they might receive from the long-distance parent. The advice comes unsolicited and the local parent resents even having to respond to it. One local father I spoke with complained about his ex-partner criticizing him for how he handled a situation with their daughter.

> I know I'm not perfect, but I do my best and I don't need her telling me how to be a parent, especially

when she's so far away and she didn't choose to hang around and help me be a parent.—Harold

Harold needs to tell his ex-wife that he doesn't appreciate what he feels is her intrusive behavior. He'd like to hear from her, every once in a while, that she notices he is doing a good job with their daughter, and then maybe he'd be able to hear the criticism.

Parents in general are very vulnerable to criticism. Divorced parents are especially sensitive to any accusations of wrongdoing concerning their children. When long distances complicate the relationship between ex-mates, even greater consideration needs to be given regarding how both the local and the long-distance parent would feel being judged by the other.

Robin initiated therapy with me because she felt increasingly shut out of her children's lives and wanted help to correct this very painful situation. Due to circumstances that she felt were truly beyond her control (illness and financial troubles), she felt forced to relinquish custody of her children to her ex-husband. She had to move back to her parents' house, which was nine hundred miles away from where her children and ex-husband now lived. Robin would do anything and everything to stay in touch with her children, but her ex-husband became more and more resentful of her involvement. He didn't want to talk to her so much and he didn't like filling her in on all the details of their children's lives. Her questions were irritating to him—he felt as if he had enough to cope with without her endless worries, and he finally told her that if she was really that concerned about the kids, she could move back and live closer to them.

What Robin really wanted from her ex-husband that he was unable or unwilling to provide was a means to an intimate relationship with her faraway children. She felt very guilty about not being able to be a full-time mother and in some way hoped that her long, drawn-out conversations with him would help to satisfy the longing and pain she had about being away from her children. It didn't work, though, and within a short time, proved more counterproductive for Robin.

In therapy, Robin was able to express her deep sorrow at being away from her children. "The day I had to move away from them was the day I literally thought I would die," she said. She mourned their loss and then began to make some realistic goals for how she could strengthen her relationship with her children and be more supportive of her ex-husband. Robin told her ex-husband that she was extremely grateful to him for taking such good care of the children, which she was. Instead of pumping him for details, she started to ask the children directly what their days were like and found that talking with them was actually more satisfying to her. Robin realized that part of being a long-distance parent included letting go in some ways and that she was never going to know every detail of their lives. That is one of the harsh realities for long-distance parents and for their children.

Robin's ex-husband responded very positively to her change in behavior and soon began asking for her advice in regard to the children. What was once an antagonistic relationship turned into a rather friendly one, which was certainly healthier for everyone involved.

Although long-distance parents are not usually involved in their children's daily lives, they can play a unique role because of their distance. That is, they can be more objective observers of the interactions between the local parent and the child and use that objectivity to help negotiate quarrels or misunderstandings. While this special role doesn't exactly compensate for all that the long-distance parent misses, the assistance can be invaluable for those on the home front.

One of the ways in which I have been able to be supportive to Jeff long-distance is as an intermediary in disputes between him and Josh. They don't happen often and I don't always know about them, but when I do, I intercede. In a phone conversation with Josh about a year ago, he told me he was furious at his dad for not trusting him to take care of something. I encouraged him to talk to his dad and explain his side of things and he said he wasn't willing to do that. I then got Jeff on the phone; he was furious at Josh for exploding at him in what he thought was an inappropriate manner. Jeff didn't think he deserved such an outburst. I started talking with Jeff about the highs and lows of adolescent emotions, and the anger and outbursts that other parents have with their adolescents on a fairly regular basis. Jeff needed to set limits with Josh, giving him a solid grounding in reality by letting Josh know when he was overreacting. At this point, Jeff was still too angry at Josh to want to talk with him either. I encouraged him to talk to Josh sooner rather than later, on the "life is short" theory. I told Jeff that I appreciated him for knowing how to work things out with Josh and for caring enough to do so. A short time later I got a call from Josh saying that he and his dad had talked things over and everything was fine now. A few days later I got a note from Jeff thanking me for my "enormously supportive words" during a time of high emotion. I, the long-distance parent, out of the direct line of fire, really helped ease a tense situation and of course I was very pleased to be able to contribute to the mental health of my family. My relationship with Jeff was solid enough that I could give him some advice and he could take it. We rely on each other for that and have come through for each other many times over the years.

Marjorie, whose fourteen-year-old daughter lives with her, tells a different story. After eight years of trying to settle her differences with her ex-husband, she has resigned herself to being a parent who has no partnership with her child's father. There is virtually no communication between her and her ex-husband. Her daughter makes all the arrangements to see her father. "My ex-husband is into a very free life-style and he doesn't want any responsibility," says Marjorie. He doesn't want to talk to Marjorie if they have a difference of opinion concerning their daughter. He doesn't want to work on a regular basis and contribute any child support regularly. He says he loves his daughter, sees her at least twice a year, and sends Marjorie money when he can. Marjorie, left feeling very alone raising her daughter after years of squabbling, has come to the realization that nothing is going to change. For years, she would call her ex-husband and try to engage him in discussions about their daughter, but he made it clear that he was just not interested in hearing from her. He was interested, though, in having Marjorie share in transportation costs when their daughter came to visit him. Not wanting to deprive her daughter of a relationship with her father, Marjorie agreed to share in those costs, even though he did not meet his financial responsibility to her throughout the years. She put a stop to this recently. If her ex-husband wants to see his daughter, he will pay the full cost. If he does not, he won't see his daughter. Of course there is a price to pay, and their daughter is the one who will suffer, but Marjorie feels she has paid much more than her share already.

The majority of long-distance relationships between parents go much more smoothly than Marjorie's. For the most part, ex-partners have been able to maintain some degree of civility between them and have been able to work out their finances and support for the children on a more equitable basis. One custodial mother I spoke with felt that her child's relationship with her long-distance father was more important than pressing him to pay child support.

Shari's father had agreed to pay child support of thirty dollars per week but did so only last year. The first three years we were apart he gave essentially nothing. This past year he has contributed ten dollars a week. I pay all the bills. However, I feel that Shari having a warm relationship with her father is the central issue so I have not done much about this.—Fran

The central issue is that Shari's father needs to contribute more financially, as well as have a loving relationship with his daughter. The two are not mutually exclusive.

Fran feels that if she fought for more child support, Shari's relationship with her father would suffer. Fran is concerned that he would withdraw altogether. As a therapist, my concern is that, unconsciously, Fran is teaching her daughter that men are irresponsible, that you can't count on them, and that men don't come through for women. Fran needs to tell her ex-husband that it's harmful for her daughter to see him in this light. Fran would be doing her daughter a big favor by demanding more child support from her father. Shari would then see her mother as strong and able to take care of her needs.

I have always shared in the financial responsibilities of raising my son. When his father and I first separated, I contributed a portion of my income to Josh's support, and as my income increased, my contribution to his support increased. (In an earlier book, *Joint Custody and Co-Parenting,* I discuss the philosophy of each parent contributing to the child's financial support according to each of their abilities to pay.) When Josh moved to Vermont with his father, I contributed to his care on a monthly basis and have done so regularly.

On the Mother's Day before Josh moved, my ex-husband gave me a very special gift. It was a thousand dollars, to be used toward transportation costs so that money would not interfere with Josh and me seeing each other. That had been a major concern of mine—that I would not be able to afford to see Josh on a regular basis. But thanks to Jeff's generosity and the low air fares then available, I was able to see Josh approximately once a month for the first year he lived in Vermont.

What financial arrangements have you made with your ex-partner? If you are the long-distance parent, do you contribute financial support? Many long-distance mothers I have spoken with are proud of the financial contribution they make to the care of their children. Christine's son lives in England with his father and she lives in New York. It was Christine who made the decision that her son, who was then seven, live with his father. Scott is now sixteen, doing very well, and Christine feels she made the right decision by having her son live with his father. ''I have always contributed to his care, paying for my share of Scott going to boarding school, I pay for his semiannual trips to the States, I contribute extras all the time, and I wouldn't have it any other way.''

Christine and her ex-husband have come to a mutual understanding over the years. There was tremendous bitterness at first, with her ex-husband kidnapping Scott and taking him back to England. Christine fought for custody in Old Bailey and the battle wore on for a long time. She won, but after several very difficult years in the States, she felt her son would be better off with his strict disciplinarian of a father. Christine relinquished custody to her ex-husband and has maintained a fairly good relationship with him since that time.

> I specified what I wanted for Scott as far as schooling went, but I had to leave it in my ex-husband's hands. I trust him pretty much. We do okay together—we will always be in touch.

Christine is usually not called in a crisis, but she does hear about crises after the fact from her ex-husband. She feels there's not much she can do because she's so far away, and she relies on her ex-husband to handle the situation appropriately. As often as she can, she deals directly with Scott. She makes all travel arrangements with him and sends Scott the money and tickets for his trips to visit her.

Another relationship that has gone through many alterations over the years is the one that John, a long-distance parent of three years, has with his ex-wife, Janice. Their separation was a fairly amicable one: Janice moved with their daughter Vanessa to a nearby location and John saw his daughter whenever he wished. Janice then remarried and John established a fairly friendly relationship with Vanessa's stepfather. Although Janice had promised to pay her half of the bills she and John had accumulated together, she did not do so and John did not press the matter. After about a year, John was told that Janice, her new husband, Carl, and Vanessa were moving to South Carolina. The decision was presented to him as a *fait accompli*. He wasn't asked how he felt about it (John feels that Janice knew how upset he would be and decided not to tell him earlier), and he wasn't given much advance warning. "It wasn't like one night they were gone and I didn't know where they were. But it was, BOOM! We're moving to South Carolina. Good-bye."

John started having a very hard time. He lost his job, was trying every way he could to find work; he still had mortgage payments and a lot of debts that had been accumulated in his marriage. He fell a little behind in child support.

I got a letter served on me from South Carolina that Janice was suing me for child support. She never kept her part of the agreement in paying her share of the bills we had. I really felt like it was a knife in the back. Now it's court-enforced. I don't need it court-enforced. I always gave her everything I could.

Now John's child support check goes out every two weeks and he is still resentful of the need for this arrangement. When Janice and Carl moved, they asked John to allow Carl to adopt Vanessa and said then he would no longer have to pay child support. John would not hear of this and was insulted at the suggestion. Nevertheless John and Janice have been on mostly friendly terms. John does not do anything to alienate his ex-wife and she, in turn, has tried to make things easier for him. She encourages Vanessa to call her father and supports their relationship in every way she can. Janice calls upon John for advice and guidance in raising their daughter and has recently told John that he's been a very good friend to her over the years.

John's position with his ex-wife has been to suppress his own feelings and be pleasant with her. He wants to have free and easy access to his daughter, he wants to be included as much as possible in her upbringing, and he doesn't want to have arguments and upsets long-distance. He feels his approach has worked for him. His relationship with Vanessa is closer than ever and now that she is a teenager, he needs his ex-wife less and less to help him maintain a strong bond with his daughter.

There is a fine line between suppressing your own anger and hurt in order to keep your relationship running smoothly with your ex-partner and consequently with your long-distance children, and not allowing yourself to feel as though you've been used. How you walk that line will depend on the kind of relationship you have with your ex-partner and whether you can discuss delicate matters, such as your feelings, with the other parent.

Constance Ahrons, Ph.D., associate director of the Marriage and Family Therapy Program at the University of Southern California and author of *Divorced Families,* feels that the relationship between the ex-partners is critical. "How much the local parent supports the relationship with the long-distance parent is the extent to which the parent-child bond will be encouraged and strengthened," says Dr. Ahrons.

You need to decide for yourself what you are willing to do to have that happen. If you have managed to ride out the early bitter years after a divorce to develop a more neutral or friendly relationship with your ex-partner, your relationship with your long-distance child will reap the benefits. On the other hand, if you are still embroiled in a hostile, frustrating relationship with your ex-mate, you and your long-distance child may find your relationship frought with obstacles to overcome.

Leo has decided, after years of wrangling with his ex-wife, to cease and desist. He does not call his former home anymore and has suspended his efforts to have a relationship with his son. He is waiting for his son to attend college next fall in order to contact him. The years without his son have been grueling for Leo. He has tried in every way he knew how to contact his son independently of his ex-wife, but his son was unresponsive as well. He got no answers to his letters, which he mailed certified and return-receipt requested, his phone calls were blocked, and his checks went uncashed. He tried using friends and relatives to deliver messages to his son. He spoke to the school principal and guidance counselor, but they did not want to interfere or give Leo any information about his son. He went to his son's hometown and waited for him outside of school, but never saw him coming down the steps. It had been so many years since he had seen his boy that he probably didn't recognize him. He waited in his van, parked outside his son's house, but someone, probably his ex-wife, called the police and had him gently ushered out of town. He hasn't given up forever, but he has given up for now.

Leo's ex-wife has literally prevented him from having a relationship with his son, and since his son is angry at him in his own right for having deserted him at the age of six, virtually any relationship Leo has tried to maintain over the years has been thwarted.

There are no excuses, of course, for Leo's not contacting his son for years. Although he blames his ex-wife for turning his son against him, it was his own neglect that caused this break in their relationship. When Leo and his wife separated, Leo wanted to become a writer. He wanted to leave his job and go back to school. He was told by his lawyer that in order to avoid being sued for child support, he'd have to leave the state. His therapist at the time also agreed with this plan. Neither man, reports Leo, ever once considered what this scheme would do to his relationship with his son. Neither man ever once even brought it up. Of course, it didn't occur to Leo to think about it either. Years later, through therapy, Leo has come to see that he was doing to his son what his father had done to him—abandoning him at an early age.

Leo has a lot of repair work to do in the future. He has given up hope of ever having a civil relationship with his ex-wife and is not too optimistic about getting a response from his son. But he will continue to strive for that. He hopes that when his son no longer lives with his mother, he will be more open to knowing his father. It's a long shot, but it's the only one Leo has right now.

I have written about the varieties of relationships that ex-partners fashion for themselves over time and how they do or don't support each other's long-distance relationship with their child. For the most part, the long-distance parents I interviewed were able to maintain neutral to friendly relationships with their ex-mates, although, to be sure, there were problems to surmount. They wanted their child to have a strong relationship with both parents and knew that their cooperation with one another would allow this to be a much smoother process for them and for their child. My own relationship with my long-distance family has continued to grow and change over the years. When Josh graduated from high school last June, we all came together to celebrate the occasion. Of course I was there, along with my present husband, Herb. My parents flew up from New York for the event, and Jeff and his wife, Nicandra, were our hosts. My parents had seen Jeff on occasion since our divorce fourteen years ago, but it was the first time they had been at Jeff's home.

The weekend went very well. We all ate out together, Jeff and Nicandra made a delicious dinner for everyone on another night, and we did what we set out to do, which was to celebrate Josh and share in our pride in his accomplishments. I had written a song for the occasion, which we all sang, toasts were made, and no one looking in on us would have known the intricacies of relationships present that weekend. Herb and I stayed with Jeff and Nicandra, as I have done during all of my visits to see Josh in Vermont. I have always been welcomed in their home and they in mine.

Most people think the relationship I have with my ex-husband is unusual. Most ex-partners do not feel comfortable spending the night in each other's homes, especially with new spouses along. What is important to me is that my relationship with Jeff has been instrumental in helping me strengthen the bond I have with Josh. Jeff has supported my relationship with Josh completely, and has done everything he could to assist me in being a strong, involved parent. For his part, Jeff has had my support and partnership around Josh over the past four years and, he says, "It has made a big difference to me in not feeling alone as a parent. I have a sense that you really appreciate that I am doing a good job in raising your son in the absence of your being on location."

My advice, then, is to nurture a relationship with a minimum of conflict. If you cannot be friendly, being neutral with each other in the face of unspoken resentments will help assure that your long-distance child will not be caught between two parents at war. If you can be cooperative and communicate often with each other about your child's needs, you as the long-distance parent will be grateful and the local parent will get much-needed support. If you maintain a relationship with your ex-partner that encourages you to be the best parents you can be to your child, then your child will experience the best of both of you in an inherently difficult situation.

CHAPTER 5

What About the Children?

No one likes long-distance parenting, especially the children. They are adamant about NOT liking it. They speak very poignantly about the pain of being separated from a parent. Some feel the hurt more than others. Some have had a more difficult time adjusting to the separation than others. Some have managed to deny a lot of their sadness and avoid thinking about it most of the time. But all of them would like their situations to be different. All of them speak negatively about having long-distance parents.

> I know my mother thought it was best, but when she made me move with her, away from my dad, it was the worst thing that ever happened to me. It was very cruel of her and I don't know if I'll ever be able to forgive her.—Jason, age sixteen

> The other kids think I have a great life because I get to go to California three times a year. It's not a great life to be away from your mom for most of the year. As a matter of fact, it stinks.—Satya, age fifteen

> I've been very angry and upset and hurt just because my dad is not around. He is really ignorant about my daily life.—Julian, age fifteen

> I was sad for a long time but now I don't mind it so much because I've been living apart from my dad for so long.—Naomi, age eight

Mostly at night is when I miss my mom most. We used to sit around and talk a lot and of course we can't do that anymore.—Chrissa, age twelve

The comments made about having a long-distance parent all reflect the pathos, anguish, and deep sadness these children feel. The loss and feeling of being abandoned are evident; it cannot be hidden. For some children, the loss is couched in terms of endearment. Others wear their pain for everyone to see. Children talk about the unfairness of it all, about having to span two coasts in order to get their rightful dose of two parents. Children of long-distance parents have to relinquish one parent in order to be with the other. They are always sad to be leaving one parent or happy to see the other. There is sadness and loss connected with every reunion with their other parent.

Elana, a seventeen-year-old who has been traveling from the East Coast to the West for the past thirteen years, describes how she used to feel "total anguish and sorrow" boarding the plane because she was leaving one parent. On the plane, she felt nothing. Then she'd experience "total happiness" as she got nearer her destination.

Now I have sadness and happiness inside me all the time. It's always with me. Now when I get on the plane I'm sad to be leaving and happy to be going, right away.

Elana will be going away to college next year, leaving both parents. How will she decide where to spend her vacations and summers? It's always been so clear-cut before. She lives with her mom during the school year, and all vacation time is spent with her father. Elana is envious of her friends whose parents, while they might be divorced, at least live fairly close to each other. She can't drop over to see her dad for a few hours, the way some of her friends can. Her friends, however, envy her relationship with her parents. Elana is close to both of them, something she feels is a rarity among her friends. "My friends who have parents living close to each other are closer with the parent they live with. Being a long-distance kid, I am equally close with both my parents." She makes the most of her time with her father and has worked on keeping in close contact with him. "I take my responsibilities to my parents very seriously. Maybe I'm warped, but I love both my parents an awful lot."

Elana was supposed to spend the last two years of high school with her dad, but when it came time to make the change, she didn't want to move. She did want to spend more time with her dad. She also felt she had worked hard all her life to do well in school and to get into a good college and didn't want to risk changing schools in the crucial junior and senior high school years.

There had been too much upheaval in my life. My mom and I moved around a lot, and when she remarried for the third time I finally had roots, actually in the ground. I didn't know how I'd react to a new environment so I decided to stay with my mom and finish school. It was rough on my dad but he did understand.

Most children are not given the choice of where they will live when one parent moves far away. It is only later, when they get older, that they begin to voice a preference. Jason, age sixteen, knew at the outset that he didn't want to move away from his dad. His mother insisted that he move back East with her two and a half years ago, along with two other children. Jason's world fell apart. Not only was he no longer with his dad, but he was uprooted from his friends, who meant a great deal to him. "I had absolutely no say in the matter. At first the situation was unbearable. It was like going from paradise to hell overnight.''

Jason missed his father terribly, and while his extreme despair has eased somewhat over the intervening years, he still longs for his father and looks forward to the time he can return to attend college in California, so he can be closer to him. Some of the hardest times for Jason have been when people around him began to be unsympathetic to his pain at being away from his dad. He doesn't like being told that he has to adjust and learn to like his situation. He especially doesn't like hearing, ''Life isn't fair.'' Jason is all too well aware of that and feels that unless people have gone through the same experience, they can never understand just how difficult it is for him. He is making an effort to adjust to his situation, but his sadness still overwhelms him at times. ''It takes time. It takes time. The sadness lasts for a very long time, and once in a while,'' says Jason, ''it eases up a little.''

Jason's mother, Nina, suffered along with her son. She felt tremendously guilty for the pain she was causing Jason, and although the move was a positive one for her and her two older children, Jason's difficult adjustment caused her many doubts about the decision she made to move. Nina made every effort to encourage Jason to accept and become involved in his new life, but it was many years before he regained some of his self-confidence by making new friends and doing well in school.

When one parent makes a decision to move and take the children along, we can assume that the move will be a major upheaval in their lives. If the children have had any relationship with the parent left behind, they may feel very cut off and isolated in their new surroundings. If the connection to the long-distance parent is a strong one, the child may voice his disagreement with the move; but when he is forced to go, he still feels powerless to affect any different outcome. He is left feeling angry and frustrated.

Jason's mother experienced the brunt of his anger.

Although she considered allowing Jason to stay with his father, she didn't feel Jason would be well cared for by his father, either emotionally or financially. She also did not want to split up the family and leave Jason behind while she took her other two children with her. Nina has gotten professional help for herself and her family. She has learned to listen to Jason and really hear his pain and rage. She has also learned that there are times when she does not want to hear about how miserable she has made his life and that she needs to help him focus on his life in the present. In time, Jason will need to deal with his feelings toward his father for not having the resources to care for him. By not having his own life in order, Jason's father made it easy for Jason to move. He could not fight for his son and, in his own way, abandoned him.

Children don't live their lives in a vacuum, separate from the other people around them. Rather, they are part of a larger system, which includes their parents, siblings, stepparents, stepsiblings, other relatives, friends, and so on. What is going on in that system that either helps or hinders children in their adjustment to long-distance relating with one parent? Why do some children seem to adjust fairly easily to a difficult situation, or with minimal pain, while others bemoan their fate for years and never seem to make peace with their situation?

These questions cannot be answered simply. Each family is unique and its responses to life's challenges are quite individual. A child who is having major difficulty being without his dad may be acting out the incomplete relationship between his parents. Perhaps the parents are divorced in legal document only, and their relationship is still fraught with emotional entanglements; the child feels this tension and it is unsettling for him. Perhaps the struggle between his parents is evident every time his dad calls. He may feel caught in a tug of war, in the middle of his parents' battle. Where does his loyalty lie? The child probably experienced these feelings before the divorce took place, but now that there is a physical separation as well, he may feel literally ripped apart. Physical distance tends to dramatize very clearly what was already present in family relationships.

Another child who feels lost is Mavis, age twelve. "My mother? She moved away to remarry and start a new life and kind of forgot about me." Mavis was five when her parents divorced. Her mother moved out of the house and lived nearby for the next several years; Mavis saw her mother frequently and her parents seemed to get along reasonably well. They never fought about who would have Mavis and Mavis thought she was fairly lucky, all things considered, since she got to see both her parents whenever she wanted to. During the course of her work, Mavis' mother, Susan, met a man who lived fifteen hundred miles away. For the next several years, Susan had a long-distance romance, and although she was well aware of the possible consequences of this alliance—that is, she would move away from her only child—Susan slowly pursued this relationship. Two years ago, Susan did remarry and moved to another part of the country to live with her new husband; to hear Mavis tell it, Susan has all but forgotten that she had a daughter.

Mavis is very bitter. While her father is good to her and she gets along all right with her new stepmother, she misses her own mother very much and often cries herself to sleep at night. Mavis sees her mother two or three times a year. They talk on the phone about twice a week and Susan writes letters and cards to Mavis on a regular basis. Still, Mavis feels as if she's been abandoned. There are no words to console her; there is nothing her mother can say that eases Mavis' sorrow. Mavis thinks that her mother will have another baby soon and that she will become even less important to her mom than she already is now. Mavis describes her basic feeling as having a "steady ache in my heart." She goes about her business, does well in school, has friends and a busy schedule, yet she is not a lighthearted twelve-year-old. She feels uncomfortable talking to her stepmother about boys, but her mother is too far away to help her. Mavis is lonely, feels very cut off from her mother, and while she has begun to accept the situation as her fate, she does not like it at all.

> I tell my mom how I feel and she listens to me, but there's really nothing she can do for me. Unless she's willing to move back here, nothing will really change.

Susan needs to talk to Mavis about the reality of the situation and the fact that she is not going to move back to her hometown. Susan also needs to be prepared to go over and over the same painful feelings with Mavis; once is not nearly enough. Susan needs to reassure Mavis that she loves her very much and she will always be her number-one girl. Now that Mavis is getting older, Susan should be open to the possibility of Mavis coming to live with her for her high school years. Teenagers very often want to live with their same-sex parent, and while this would be a drastic change for Mavis, it might be one that would be a healthy resolution to this seemingly unresolvable conflict.

Not all children of long-distance parents are unhappy. But most children of long-distance parents have had to work extra-hard at adjusting to a very difficult situation. Julian, age fifteen, says that initially he was very hurt and angry that his father wasn't around. "Then I went through a stage of living my own life and not paying much attention to him. Never calling him, just waiting for him to call. Right now I'm angry at the situation, but I understand it." Julian has had a long-distance father for eight years.

Dara, age five, has never known anything but a long-distance life; her parents have never lived together. Here is Dara's description of having a long-distance father:

> I want my daddy to live with me because I miss him when I don't get to see him. Then when I see my daddy I really am happy because I haven't seen him for a very long time. Then I go off and play when he leaves because I cry when he leaves.

Oliver, age seven, had a very difficult time adjusting to his parents' divorce. At first, his father moved to the Caribbean and Oliver stayed with his mother. He missed his father terribly. He began having problems at school and fought with his mother. Oliver's father then moved to California and as soon as Oliver went there to visit, he calmed down considerably. It was decided that Oliver would stay with his father, who has since remarried and moved to Ohio. Oliver flics to Philadelphia twice a month to visit his mother and speaks to her on the phone twice a week.

Oliver wants his mother and father to live together again, which is a request that most children of divorce make, even years after their parents divorce. "If my parents don't live together, then I want everyone in my family to live together—my parents, my stepmom and my two stepbrothers. And then I'd like my mom to get married again so I would have two daddies and two mommies. I worry about my mom living alone." Oliver spends a lot of time trying to figure out family relationships. He asks his mother a lot of questions about why she and his father divorced. He wants to know if his mom likes his stepmom. He hates saying good-bye to his mom every other weekend and wonders why she can't come to Ohio to live. Oliver is doing everything he knows how to do to make some sense of why his parents live far away from each other.

An important factor in the satisfactory adjustment of children to life without a significant other, a parent, is how well they get along with a possible new stepparent and stepsiblings. Oliver does get along with his stepmother, yet can you imagine the distress a child would feel who no longer lives near his mom, yet lives in a household with a new stepmother with whom he does not get along? The daily wear and tear on everyone's nerves is enormous.

Even if the child and his stepmother do get along, they may be virtual strangers to one another and thrown into living together without benefit of courtship, so to speak. Oliver's new stepbrother may not welcome his arrival into his home, not to mention his room. This would put Oliver in an extremely awkward position, one that would make his adjustment to living without his mom all the more difficult. These issues and more concerning remarriage and long-distance relationships will be discussed in Chapter 7.

Vanessa, age sixteen, whom we met in the previous chapter, moved with her mother and stepfather to South Carolina five years ago. At first, she had a hard time getting used to life without her father, who lives in Texas. But now, she feels she has adjusted pretty well to the situation. In fact, Vanessa feels she has a better relationship with her father long-distance than she would if they were still living in the same town.

My dad and I are closer because we're apart. It would be more of a strain if we were together. My faults would be more noticeable to him and his would be to me. This way, we do not take each other for granted. We take the time to talk, to know each other.

Vanessa works hard at maintaining a close relationship with her dad. She keeps him informed of what's going on in her life. "It makes me feel really good to know that he's interested in the little things," she says. Sharing the little things also has painful consequences for Vanessa. Her dad follows her school interests very closely and encourages Vanessa to get involved with the school newspaper. When Vanessa was appointed editor of the paper, her dad didn't get to see the happiness "right there on my face." He didn't get to share in the excitement with her, right at that moment. Not being together to share the "good news times," as Vanessa says, has made her feel very sad on numerous occasions.

But Vanessa's overall attitude is a positive one. Even at the point of saying good-bye after a visit, which is an extremely difficult time for most long-distance parents and their children, Vanessa tells herself that she knows she'll see her dad again and that "this won't be the last good-bye." The only time Vanessa remembers crying at the end of a visit was when her dad gave her his construction hat to wear as she boarded the plane. "That hat was part of him. He wore it all the time on the job. That really broke me up, but I'm very proud to have that hat."

Reunions and good-byes are often the central focus of long-distance relationships, especially in the beginning when the separation first occurs. "When will I see my mom again?" "How will I stop myself from crying on the plane going back home?" The pain that parents feel at the time of separation from a child is the same pain the child feels. Children experience all the anguish, sorrow, and loss that adults feel. The separation, especially at the time of saying good-bye, is heartfelt.

My stepdaughter, Satya, has said many good-byes to her parents as she flies between coasts to visit them. Satya is now fifteen and has lived on the East Coast with her dad (my husband Herb) and me since she was nine years old. She did spend one year with her mother in California, when she was thirteen. She, like Vanessa, tries to maintain a positive attitude in the face of a painful situation. "I feel like crying a lot, but I don't. My mom cries and my dad cries whenever we have to say good-bye. Later, when I think about it more and realize that one of them is gone, I feel bad all over again." For Satya, the most difficult part of having a long-distance mom is that her mom doesn't know what she's doing on a daily basis. This leaves Satya feeling cut off from her mom and that they are not as close as she would like them to be. Satya's friends in school ask her why she's not with her mom in California; Satya doesn't want to get into the whole story. She loves being with her dad— they've always been exceptionally close—but she hates East Coast weather. It's not a simple answer, but she doesn't think people are really interested in the details, anyway. What her friends know is that it sounds great to live in California but Satya is living in Philadelphia, instead. It doesn't make sense to them, and it hardly makes sense to Satya.

Another teenage girl trying to make some sense out of living away from her mother is Kelly. "When I say good-bye to my mom," says Kelly, age fourteen, "I kind of make believe that I'm just going from her house to my dad's house in the same town, like I used to. I don't think that it's three-thousand miles away now. I just say, 'I'll talk to you tonight,' and that's it. We try to keep it light."

Kelly and her mom have been separated for less than a year. She presently lives with her dad and stepmother and is making plans to join her mom and new stepfather in Oregon this summer to complete her last three years of high school. One of the hardest parts for Kelly is that when her mom moved away, that meant the house she grew up in was sold. "The blossoming crab apple tree in the front yard, our favorite, was cut down by the new owner. My safe, secure, childhood home is gone." Kelly's safe, secure childhood is also gone. Even though her parents divorced, they remained in the same geographical area and Kelly lived with each of them half the time. The transition from one two-parent home to two one-parent homes was manageable for Kelly. Now that one parent has moved far away, the evidence of her parents' divorce is more noticeable to Kelly, and more painful. "When I used to go back and forth between two homes, my mother would always tell me she's only a phone call away if I really need her. Now she still tells me that, only it'll take her six hours to get to me, not six minutes."

When Kelly moves to Oregon, she will be leaving her dad and stepmother and saying good-bye to friends she's had her whole life. Still, she is excited about being with her mom and doesn't want to dwell at all on the negative aspects of the move. Her dad has assured her that they will be in touch often, plans are already made for some return trips home, and Kelly is looking forward to her new life out West.

It is important for both the local parent and the long-distance parent to be involved in helping the child adjust to her new circumstances. How does the child's larger system operate to either support her in her new life or prevent her from making a satisfactory adjustment? Both parents need to look at themselves as individuals and as the parental unit to answer this question. If there are stepparents, as in Kelly's family, they, too, need to be involved in the planning for a move, with the major responsibility taken by the child's parents.

Rick, age thirteen, says he misses his father most when he does something he is proud of and doesn't get to share it personally with his dad. He feels most alone at those times, most cut off from his dad. Rick and his dad did not have a strong relationship when they lived in the same house. It was only after his parents' divorce that Rick's dad began taking a stronger interest in him. Rick feels that as a result of the divorce, he lost his dad living at home with him, but he gained a much closer relationship with him, even if that relationship spans a continent. Rick's dad moved from Chicago to Alaska and Rick is the only kid he knows who spends most of the summer in Alaska. On rare occasions, Rick has flown up to Alaska for the Christmas holidays, but mostly his time with his dad is during the summer. ''I wait all year long for summertime to come. I don't even mind the wait anymore. It's part of the excitement for me.'' During the year, Rick and his dad write and talk on the phone about what they did together last summer and what they're going to do together this summer. Their relationship, Rick says, gets better and better. He doesn't like the idea that his dad lives so far away, but he's not complaining. When Rick has to say good-bye to his dad at the end of his summer visit, he starts talking to himself about a week ahead of time, telling himself that the year will go by fast and he'll be back before he knows it. All that talking, Rick says, does him no good. When he has to board the plane, he cries anyhow and feels just awful. ''There is nothing that my father or my mother or anyone can say to me that can take away that awful feeling. I just know it takes time for me to start feeling better.'' Rick likes to arrive home a day or two before school starts, so he can quickly get back into the scheme of things.

Many children who spend a long period of time with their long-distance parent find the transition time back into their "regular lives" a difficult one. They have to get used to a different routine, often different schedules, different rules. Mostly what they have to get used to is life without their other parent. For some who have friends and a whole other life with their long-distance parent, the transition is even more painful. When Jason goes to visit his dad in California, where he used to live, he also visits his old, good friends. When he says good-bye to his dad, he also says good-bye to his friends. This makes him even more aware of the life he used to have and that since he's moved away, he hasn't developed a close network of friends in his new city.

Satya, too, has a very close group of friends in California, and she doesn't feel that connection to friends in Philadelphia. Are these children holding on to their lives in their previous communities in such a way that it prevents them from making new friends once they've moved? When children move, whether the move is of their own choosing or not, the decision to make their new community their home, and invest themselves there, is often a slow and arduous process.

My son, Josh, chose to move to Vermont with his dad, yet he remained very resistant to accepting Vermont as his new home. He began to idealize Philadelphia in his mind. He would call me and plaintively ask, "Can I come home now?" He decided that he didn't "fit" in Vermont and had his teachers agreeing with him that his new school was a difficult one to fit into as an outsider. Somewhere between six months and a year after moving to Vermont, Josh began to make some friends. But it still took even longer than that for him to accept Vermont as his home. In an essay he wrote for a college application on what was the greatest risk he had taken in his life, Josh wrote poignantly about his move to Vermont. He didn't see the move itself as the risk, but rather the decision to accept and make Vermont his home as the greatest risk. That would mean giving up the myth of Philadelphia being better, and realizing and understanding that he could have a satisfying life without me living nearby.

These are heady feelings for a fifteen-year-old to grapple with. "What if I decide to accept my new home and reach out to people and then they turn around and reject me?" Issues of loyalty come up. "Will mom be upset if I'm having a good time in my new life with dad?" It's not easy for children to figure out how they can accept and adjust to the dramatic changes in their lives—living without a loved parent and perhaps having experienced a move to a new location at the same time.

Parents need to help their children through this adjustment time, and both the local parent and the long-distance parent need to be involved in this process. The child's pain and loneliness need to be recognized and appreciated by his parents before he can achieve some sense of equilibrium in his life. Both parents can tell their child—on the phone, through letters and in person—that he is not alone with his feelings. "I know this is an awful time for you, son, and I'm here to help you through it. Tell me all about it." The child is experiencing feelings he's never had before—the loss of a parent nearby. Don't expect the child's sorrow to dissipate quickly. He is in mourning.

Tell children that it takes time to feel better about being apart and that while they are so unhappy right now, things *will* ease up. Tell them how you feel about being apart and what you do to help yourself diminish the pain. A supportive local parent will reassure a child that you, the long-distance parent, will do everything possible to help him see the other parent and be in touch regularly. A supportive long-distance parent will tell his daughter that it would give him great pleasure to know that she is enjoying her life.

Children need to hear that while you acknowledge

their sadness and pain now, you expect them to move on, continue to develop their own interests and friends. You may find it difficult to help your child in this way, especially if you are experiencing a great deal of guilt and feel responsible for creating this painful situation in the first place. When your child is having a hard time being without his other parent, does not seem to be adapting to the separation after a year or so, and you are not able to assist your child in making this transition, find some outside help. Counseling can be extremely helpful at this point, and the more members of the family who receive professional help the better off you all, especially your child, will be.

Can you find a support group for your child to belong to? Family Service Agencies and some schools run groups for children of divorce. While the children all may not have long-distance parents, many of the problems they are facing are alike. Talking about what it feels like to have parents who are divorced and geographically apart, as well, is an extremely valuable experience for many children. Knowing that they are not alone and that they are understood by others, especially by others in their own age group, gives children a much-needed sense of belonging.

Courtney, a shy girl of ten, moved with her mother to a new community. Making new friends had never been her strong point; she hated going to a new school and wondered if she would ever make a new friend. She didn't want to move in the first place, but her parents didn't give her a choice in the matter. Courtney was never particularly close with her dad, but she did miss him once they were apart. Her dad would call her from time to time, her mom was busy establishing herself in a new career, and Courtney felt left by the wayside.

When Courtney was twelve, she ran away from home. She didn't run far, but it was a clear statement to her parents that she was not coping with her new life and that she needed help. Her mom called her dad and for the first time in years they were cooperating with each other, figuring out how to help their daughter. After some initial blaming and defensiveness, both parents saw that in their own way, they were each neglecting Courtney. In speaking with the school guidance counselor, Courtney's mom discovered a group for children of divorce at a local community center. She took time off from work, brought Courtney there, and through professional help she received herself, decided to concentrate on her daughter's needs. Courtney needed more of her and more of her dad. He, in turn, became a more active dad, having Courtney visit him several times a year and calling her more often. Courtney is still shy, but she has started to make a few friends. By running away, she showed her parents what they were unable or unwilling to see for themselves—that she was an unhappy girl who could not go it alone. She brought them together in the only way she knew how and reminded each of them that they still had a daughter to care for.

There are specific times in a long-distance child's life when he particularly misses his long-distance parent. When children have a fight with their local parent, thoughts of their long-distance parent come especially to mind. They miss someone else around to soften the blow, someone else around to go to for solace and comfort in the storm. Naomi, age eight, says that she misses her dad most when "my mom gets mad at me and when I get scared or when something bad happens like when I fall and hurt myself." Naomi feels close to her dad, even though her visits with him over the past five years have been very scarce. Kelly misses her mom when her friends, who knew her mom well, start talking about what a great mom she has. Josh says the time he misses me most is when he can't get a good hug when he needs it. Alyssa, age six, says that she misses her dad most when she is away from her own home, traveling with her mom someplace. Alyssa can't explain why this is so for her. She just knows that she always thinks of her dad in those situations and wishes she could be visiting with him then, instead of visiting in a new place. Vanessa talked about a certain kind of music that will remind her of her dad. Sometimes she purposely puts on Pink Floyd or Led Zeppelin to remind her of the times she and her dad have spent together, even though she knows it will make her miss him even more.

It's the shared memories, the experiences that parents and children have together that bring forth happiness and sadness when they are separated. When I hear a certain song that reminds me of Josh, because we sang it together or enjoyed hearing it on the radio together, I am immediately reminded of the specialness of our relationship. I am filled with love for him and, almost instantly, feel a longing and a wish that we could be together right this second. Children experience the same longing. Does that ever go away? I don't think so. Some children learn better than others how to cope with that longing, how to overcome it. But it is there for every child who has been separated from a parent prematurely.

All children of divorce have experienced this premature separation and disruption in their family life when one parent leaves home. All children of divorce feel a deep sense of loss, whether they were close to the parent who leaves home or not. Long-distance children are acutely aware of the loss and, because of the geographical distance, must be reassured that they are still loved and cherished and that *both* parents will do everything they can to make sure that the long-distance relationship is maintained.

What about a long-distance parent who, in some way, gives a child messages to remain as unhappy and sad as she is about the separation? Parents who are having a difficult time with the separation themselves might not be happy to see their children blossom and grow in the same period of time. "Why isn't my child as unhappy as I am? I guess he doesn't even notice I'm gone." Such parents communicate their misery to their child by being subtly negative when the child reports meeting new friends. The child soon learns that it is not okay with his long-distance parent to go on with his life, but rather that he should stay stuck in the depression and guilt that many children of divorce experience.

Perhaps it is the local parent who is making it difficult for the child to remain in contact with the other parent, and is therefore thwarting a satsifactory adjustment to the separation. Long-distance children need to be in regular contact with their long-distance parents. They need to know that parent still cares, and any local parent who inhibits that important communication is doing her child a major disservice.

Jordan was nine at the time his father moved away. His parents fought bitterly during their marriage and his mother was glad his father was leaving town. She made it extremely difficult for Jordan's father to contact him. Phone calls were discouraged and visits were out of the question, as far as Jordan's mother was concerned. Within a few months, Jordan's behavior became problematic. He was getting in trouble at school and disobeying his mother at home. When his mother brought Jordan to see me for therapy, he had a very tough veneer. When I told him I knew he missed his dad, however, he burst into tears and curled up into a ball. I told him I knew his mom and dad fought a lot and were still very angry at each other.

''Mom doesn't like me to talk to Dad,'' Jordan explained. He made it very clear that he wanted very much to talk to his dad and that he was angry at his mom for keeping them apart. I told Jordan that I knew there was something wrong, just as he did. I said I would do my very best to find out what was going on and that I would talk to both of his parents about it. I talked to his mother first and heard about her awful marriage. She knew Jordan missed his dad but thought he'd be better off in the long run, as she would be, if he had little to do with his father. I explained that just the opposite was true. The only way that Jordan was going to have any peace was if he was permitted to have not a minimal but a strong relationship with his father. Anything less would be robbing Jordan of a central relationship in his life; and Jordan was sure to be angry at her for interfering. I recommended a family conference to discuss Jordan's needs, with both parents present. She was not pleased to hear my views, but she listened attentively. She also agreed to let me get in touch with Jordan's father.

Jordan's father was most appreciative of my call. He knew there was something very wrong but couldn't talk to his ex-wife long enough to find out what was going on. Worst of all, he wasn't able to have a satisfactory conversation with his son. I explained what I thought Jordan needed—a close relationship with both his parents. Jordan's father was planning to make a trip to visit his son and reluctantly agreed to a family conference. Not that he didn't want to help or be involved; he just didn't want any more arguments with his ex-wife. Through several phone calls with his father, therapy sessions with Jordan and his mother, and a family conference, we were able to work out a plan with which both parents could live. Jordan would talk to his father on the phone every Saturday morning. His mother agreed not to interfere with these calls. Jordan would visit his father for four weeks in the summer and for Christmas vacation. His mother agreed to go along with this because it meant so much to Jordan.

Jordan's behavior improved dramatically. His father wanted Jordan to do well at school and expressed his anger to Jordan over the phone when he got in trouble. Jordan's father also told him to respect his mother and obey her. Jordan responded positively to his father's involvement in his life. His mother noticed the changes and was pleased that her son was calming down.

Children need to know that both their parents care about them. In Jordan's family, this meant that his mother would support his relationship with his dad, and that his dad would be in touch on a continuous basis. My professional guidance helped these parents be the best parents they could be to their child, even though they were still angry at one another.

I asked children what advice they would give to contemporaries who were soon to have a long-distance parent or who have one now. The younger children I spoke with generally agreed that it was a good idea not to worry about the situation because there wasn't much you could do about it anyway. Dara, age five, told other kids, "Don't worry, because your daddy will still love you anyway." Jordan's advice was to "talk about it when it got bad."

Adolescents tend to be more philosophical. Some voiced the opinion that if you were optimistic and worked at trying to make the best of your living situation, then things would be okay. Elana told kids to "Work at it. Don't let a separation of miles be a separation of everything else. It's hard to work at it but it's worth it." Other teenagers also took responsibility for staying in touch with their long-distance parent, feeling that they needed to reach out and let their parent know what's going on in their lives. "The worst thing to do is to let that relationship go astray," said Vanessa. "It's not easy, but you still have two parents, no matter where they live." "My friends used to think of me as strange because my dad lives far away, but now they understand that it could happen to them any time. They know that because I told them so," said Naomi.

Many children spoke of the need to wait for time to pass and then things would be better. "The first times are hard," said Jason. "The first day, week, month, year, the first birthday without my dad, the first Fourth of July. I counted them all." Kelly suggested that kids tell their parents very clearly how they're feeling about the situation and not to say that everything is fine when it's not.

Some children tend to want to take care of their parents, to protect their parents from any upset. These children, termed "parentified children," that is, children who have become parents to their own parents, will hide their own concerns at the risk of adding more burdens to their parents. From an early age, these children have been encouraged directly or indirectly to take care of the parent. Their self-worth and self-esteem are tied into their ability to take care of people. They hold on to that role for dear life because if they give that up, who are they?

Parentification starts at an early age. Divorce brings it to the fore. Loyalty issues, which are common for children of divorce, are compounded by being a parent to your own parent. The danger here is that the child does not get to be a child with someone protecting her. She gives up what she wants and needs for herself, as Kelly was suggesting when she spoke about the need for kids to tell the truth to their parents. The parentified child feels she needs to protect her parent and will say that everything is fine when it most definitely is not.

Robin was a parentified child during her parents' marriage. Her father was weak in the face of an overbearing wife and Robin was being a good little girl by taking care of him and protecting him. This was not a conscious thought, but something that a parent unconsciously develops and encourages in a child. Robin's parents divorced and her father moved away. Not only did she feel abandoned by him, but she no longer had a role in the family constellation—that of caretaker to her father. Her future relationships with men were fraught with difficulty. She was always the caretaker; men didn't come through for her and then she was always angry and disappointed. She repeated the pattern she had learned in her family as a little girl.

As parents of a child with a new long-distance parent, you can safely assume that your child is going through a troublesome time. Your child is most likely experiencing a longing for the absent parent and a deep sense of sadness that she finds difficult to express. "Brace yourself," said Jason. "There's going to be a tough road ahead."

Children need a lot of guidance and support from everyone in their network to walk down that tough road. The sense of feeling isolated and alone overwhelms some children with long-distance parents, and they need to be encouraged to share their sorrow with others. The pain is not alleviated because it is communicated; rather, what helps the child is to know he is not alone, that what he is feeling is normal, that his feelings are valid and that the hard times will pass. The pain will still recur, however, because when a child loses a parent, it hurts for a long time.

CHAPTER 6

Reunions and Good-byes

The reunions are ecstatic. You're both carnivorous—
you want to eat each other up. When my daughter
leaves? I don't even want to talk about it.—John

Both parents and children feel the pain of the separation. The pain is acute at the moment of saying good-
bye, but the feeling of loss is chronic. Parents and
children mirror each other's feelings. If you as a long-
distance parent are feeling morose about saying good-
bye, you know that your child is feeling awful as well.

For the long-distance parent, reunions and good-byes
are the initial focus of life. Your next visit is planned and
you look forward to it with great excitement. When you
first see each other, there is such exhilaration, such joy
and pleasure in just being together. Very soon you become painfully aware of the days and perhaps hours tick-
ing by until you have to say good-bye. You somehow
manage to tear yourself away from each other and then
your focus is on when you will see each other again.
There is little else of concern for the long-distance parent
when the separation first takes place.

When Josh first moved to Vermont, I could think of
little else but when I would see him again. Plans were
made well in advance so we both could look forward to
our next visit. I lead a very full life, but I would allow
nothing to stand in the way of these visits. I would leave
my new husband and stepdaughter, drive two hours from

Philadelphia to Newark Airport to catch a discount flight, and fly off to Vermont for a long weekend. As the visit was drawing near, my anticipation would begin to soar. At first, I would try to keep my excitement under control. No one else was particularly interested in my enthusiasm, and I felt somewhat foolish expressing it. So my eagerness to see Josh became a private experience. Within a day or two of the anticipated visit, I could control myself no longer and talked to my husband of my feelings. He was always very supportive of my trips to see Josh, but he had never personally experienced being separated from a child.

One of the children I interviewed said no one could understand what he was going through unless he had experienced it himself. I felt the same way. My family and close friends would try to help me get over the pain of the separation, but essentially it was a very lonely time for me. I was advised by a close friend to think of Josh as being away at boarding school. But he *wasn't* away at boarding school; he was living with his father and I wasn't there. The only time when I felt joyous during the early stages of our separation was just before I was about to see Josh and during the first glow of our reunion. Soon after we got together—and our visits were short ones—we had to face leaving each other again.

It's difficult to open and close your heart within such a short period of time. A typical scenario is this: Josh arrives here for a three-day visit. We are positively thrilled to see each other. We spend the first day being together, listening to music, taking a walk, talking constantly. I feel myself alternately clutching at him, then feeling a bit awkward and distant as you would with anyone you hadn't seen for a while. I am so proud of him, liking who he is so much. And then the thought creeps in that he'll be gone in two days. I force myself to concentrate on each moment, instead of ruining the time we do have together by worrying about it being over. I tell myself consciously that we are together now and I want to enjoy each moment we do have together. But the ache comes back again. It feels enormous in my heart. Is it the same for him, I wonder? I describe to Josh what I am feeling—the real distance in the long-distance relationship. I ask him how he handles this. He says yes, it is the same for him. He needs to protect himself somewhat, he says, from the hurt that he knows will come when we have to part again. He is fourteen years old and he knows about things like this.

Talk to your child about your feelings. If you are feeling the pain of the separation, your child will be feeling it too. I remember being very surprised during the first month Josh had moved to hear him say he missed me. I was so absorbed in my missing him, in my desolation, that I wasn't even aware of his. Of course he missed me! Children feel the counterpart to our feelings. They feel the same piercing sadness, part of which is seeing their parent being sad as well. They also mourn the loss of the relationship as it once was.

Long-distance relating is filled with feelings of emotionally soaring just before and during a reunion, and depression after a good-bye. While walking in Center City Philadelphia the other day, I ran into an acquaintance of mine whose two children live with their father in Florida. She was preparing for a ten-day visit from them, making plans, getting theater tickets, bubbly and filled with excitement. I could only envy them. Ten days! That seemed like an exorbitant amount of time to have with one's long-distance children. The longest time Josh and I have had together since he moved was five days, and that seemed like such a luxury. And at the time I saw this woman, in the height of her previsit flurry, I didn't know when I would see Josh again. He and I had been unable to make a plan for our next visit because our schedules were getting so complex. Her eager anticipation of a visit with her children was contrasted with my droopy demeanor, as I thought of a long stretch ahead without seeing Josh.

Parents who are able to spend a long period of time with their long-distance children face unique sets of

problems. When children spend the summer, or most of
it, with a long-distance parent, the transition to their other
parent's lifestyle can be a difficult one. Parent and child
must get reacquainted. The child getting off the plane
after a six-month absence may not look like the child you
said good-bye to last Christmas. Children undergo enormous growth spurts and six months may mean the difference between a chubby, preadolescent boy and a tall,
lanky teenager. One father was stunned at the physical
changes in his son. ''I didn't recognize Joey when he got
off the plane except he was still wearing the baseball cap
I had given him years ago. I guess some things never
change.''

Father and son are overjoyed to see each other. They have
stayed in close touch over the school year. Father knows
what his son's interests are and how he is doing in school.
They talk on the phone regularly, watch sports events on
TV together, and have a close relationship. Still, there's
an estrangement when they first see each other after a
long absence. They hold themselves back physically.
There's an embarrassment that they both feel. Is it okay
to be openly thrilled to be together again? Neither of
them is quite sure of how to express themselves. By now,
however, they each know that the first few days will be
awkward and then they will ease in to living together for
the summer. They have talked about this time together
beforehand. They prepare themselves for the transition
time. While they both have expectations of having a wonderful time together, they know that they have to get used
to being with each other again, that it will take some
time before they establish a comfortable level of relating.

Joey, for his part, is aware of being on his best behavior. ''There is no way that I'm going to mess up. I
watch my manners. I'm easy to get along with. I know
I'm the new kid in the house and I want everyone, especially my dad, to like me.'' Not only does Joey have
to get used to being with his dad again, he has to remember what his stepmother likes and doesn't like about his
behavior. His stepbrothers welcome him, but they make

it clear that they have to double up in a bedroom so Joey can have a room of his own. Joey feels a strain to be a perfect kid and he has learned to just grin and bear it until the first week or so passes. Then he begins to relax and be more himself, with his good points and bad points.

Joey's wisdom comes from his own experience and from being able to talk about these transition times with his dad. This is his fifth summer with his dad. One thing he *doesn't* talk about too much is the fact that while he is really very pleased to be with his dad, he finds himself missing his mom a whole lot. Dad, sensing this, feels guilty about uprooting his son and asking him to make large sacrifices so they can be together. Sometimes he feels he is asking too much of his son. There doesn't seem to be any way to get around the upheaval for Joey. Fortunately, in this situation, Joey soon eases in to his summer life. He goes to day camp with his stepbrothers, enjoys family outings with his dad and stepfamily, and is almost—not quite, but almost, accepted as a bona fide member of this family. About two weeks before the end of the summer, when the relationship between father and son is deeply rooted, it is time to think about separating. "It always breaks my heart," says Dad, "when I realize he'll be gone soon." Joey says he knows the time is coming, but he purposely plays harder at the end of the summer, so he'll be busy and won't have time to think. "The last two weeks of August is the worst time of my life. That's when I have to get ready to say good-bye again."

Younger children often have a harder time with transitions and need to be helped by their local and long-distance parent to overcome the awkwardness. They are usually more dependent on the local parent because of their age and so the leave-taking can be that much more difficult. Alia, a bright-eyed girl of seven, was planning to spend four weeks during the summer with her dad. She had not seen him since last Christmas, although they did talk on the phone regularly. About a month before

Alia's departure, she began to cling to her mother in a way she had not done previously. She wanted to sleep in her mother's bed at night and cried when it was time to go to school. Since Alia seemed pleased about visiting her dad, her mother did not connect the upcoming trip with Alia's fearful behavior. Alia's parents discussed the situation over the phone; it was her father who thought Alia might be having a hard time leaving her mom. He did not want to cancel the trip and thought his ex-wife should talk to Alia about what was going on. This was the conversation that took place between Alia and her mom.

MOM: You've been very unhappy lately, haven't you?

ALIA: Yes, I have.

MOM: Do you know why?

ALIA: No.

MOM: Well, I have a guess. I think you're unhappy about saying good-bye to me and saying hello to dad. I think it scares you.

ALIA: I'm not unhappy about saying hello to dad.

MOM: So the part about saying good-bye to me is making you unhappy.

ALIA: Yes.

MOM: Do you know why?

ALIA: I'm not sure you'll be here when I get back.

Mom went on to assure Alia that she definitely would be there upon Alia's return. In addition, she promised Alia she would talk to her twice a week when she was visiting with her dad. Dad, for his part, knew to be especially sensitive to Alia's fears and stayed very close to her when she first arrived. He held her and comforted her and talked to her about missing her mom. Within a few days after Alia's arrival, she became a bright-eyed little girl again and had a wonderful visit with her dad. She returned home to her mom, leaving her dad suffering from an acute case of heartache.

Vicki's oldest son, Gabe, lives with his father 160

miles south of her town in northern California. She and her second husband have two younger children, who live with them. When Gabe made the decision to live with his father, at age twelve, Vicki was devastated. She spent a lot of time crying and had great difficulty accepting Gabe's decision. The initial separation was a terrible time for Vicki. Even though she stayed in close contact with her son, she felt ripped apart by having one of her children live away from her. Gabe's visits home were generally good until it was time for him to leave. "He would create a major argument with some family member right before his departure. Every time!" Vicki finally realized this pattern. She knew that it was hard for Gabe to say good-bye and that by creating a fight he was making it hard in a different way. It was a diversionary tactic on Gabe's part, so he wouldn't have to deal with his own painful feelings. Vicki has helped Gabe be aware of this. She talks to him about it if she sees an argument coming on and helps him express his distress over leaving, instead of acting it out. Over time, things have gotten much easier. Vicki now feels that Gabe's decision to live with his dad was a good one in many ways; it has helped a lot to see him turn into "such a wonderful young man." The most difficult thing for Vicki about being apart from Gabe is not to be there, right away, when he needs her. A year ago, a dear friend of Gabe's was killed in a car accident and Gabe was terribly upset. Vicki could not concentrate on anything until she went down to be with him a week later. "My 'mother radar,' as I call it, just kept 'beeping' until I could be with him."

As a long-distance parent, you learn to live with the sadness of not having your child with you for many special events. Your child's birthday, or yours for instance, will probably not be celebrated together, unless it happens to fall during visiting times. A family celebration that all the aunts and uncles and cousins will attend will most likely not include your long-distance child. Father's Day, Mother's Day—these are holidays that may take on more sentimental significance for you if your child is far away.

One of the most disappointing times for a long-distance parent is when you plan a visit with your child and for some uncontrollable reason the visit has to be canceled at the last minute. One Thanksgiving, my family was planning a big dinner in New York. Josh planned to fly down from Vermont; we would pick him up in Newark on the way in to New York. We would spend the weekend in New York together, seeing the sights, going shopping, seeing a Broadway play. Josh would get to see relatives he hadn't seen in years. This glorious four-day reunion was not to be, however. On the eve of Thanksgiving, Josh came down with chicken pox. He was going nowhere.

I knew it was not a catastrophe, but it certainly felt like one to me. My husband couldn't assuage my despair. I felt a heavy weight in my heart where my joy in being with Josh should have been. When short reunions are planned and then canceled, especially around holiday times, there is no easing the feeling of loss. And that might mean a long stretch of time before you and your child get together again.

Another near-disaster was this past President's Day weekend—four days when Josh and I could free our collective schedules and be together. His eighteenth birthday had just passed, and it was his first birthday that we didn't celebrate together. So we planned a special weekend that would include a party in his honor. We'd have a musicale, in which our friends come with their musical instruments and we would all play and sing together. What came first, though, was the biggest snowstorm in a decade in New England. Flights were canceled; the Boston airport was shut down, which then delayed flights in and out of Burlington. It was not clear whether Josh would be able to fly out of Burlington at all that weekend, never mind on the day that was planned. My husband was speaking to airport personnel all over New England, we were following reports of the storm, and I was seriously feeling that unless I exerted great effort to hold myself together, I could easily go over the edge.

Perhaps I was being melodramatic, overreacting, hysterical. Josh called often, assuring me that he'd find a way to get here, that I shouldn't worry, and that everything would work out okay. I know that's the usual role of a parent speaking to a child, but this time it was Josh who kept my sinking spirits up. The day dragged on, the skies over New England were still stormy, but Josh was relentless in his desire to get here. Late in the day, he called to say there would be one flight out of Burlington to Binghamton, New York and from there he hoped to catch a flight to Philadelphia. When I finally did pick him up at the airport at seven P.M., he stumbled off a tiny commuter airline (the kind I don't like to take in good weather, never mind in times like these). Being the considerate person he is, Josh chose not to inform me that he was flying in on RinkyDink Airlines, and that he was wait-listed in Binghamton and might not make it to Philadelphia that night after all. He had originally been due to arrive at noon. It had been only a seven-hour delay but one that, at the time, seemed interminable, especially since I was never sure when the wait would be over. Seven hours out of what was only going to be four days to begin with. No, it's not tragic, but it's the stuff of heartbreak to a long-distance parent who has minimal time with a long-distance child anyway. It is not just one of those things.

The worst time for long-distance parents and kids seems to be when they have to say good-bye. Parents have expressed deep anguish when it comes time to separate after a visit. Abigail, whose son lives with his father six hundred miles away, says, ''I anticipate the depression after he leaves but I can't relieve it. I try to act normal but I don't feel normal. I have to lick my wounds alone.'' Friends often invite her out to dinner right after her son leaves, but she prefers being alone. She doesn't want to make small talk, and she doesn't want to spread her gloomy mood around. There is nothing that seems to ease the pain for Abigail except the passing of time. Many children find this is true for them as well. They don't feel like getting into the swing of things immediately after saying good-bye to their long-distance parent, but rather prefer to be by themselves, or spend quiet time with the local parent or an understanding friend. Other children and parents want to be distracted from their pain. They purposely plan to be swept up in a whirlwind of activity so that they don't have to be alone with their sorrow.

There is no right way to cope with a separation from a loved one. Experiment with various alternatives—being alone, being with a friend, being with a group of friends—and see which way feels best to you. As you have more experience saying good-bye, you might find that what felt right years ago no longer fits for you today. Your sorrow may not feel as painful and you may not need to go off by yourself.

Some parents feel a sense of relief when their long-distance children finally leave and go back home. The visit might not have gone especially well and the tension and awkwardness everyone felt at first never really dissipated. These parents experience a visit from their children as an interruption in their lives. They have to learn to make room for their children—in their hearts as well as in their homes. If the situation continues, the strain on everyone takes its toll and both long-distance parent and child wonder why they bothered getting together.

Kate is a long-distance parent who exemplifies many of these feelings. She entered therapy with me shortly after her children moved to live with their dad in Chicago. She was physically, emotionally, and financially unable to care for them adequately. Kate's world fell apart. "I didn't know who I was because if I didn't have my children to care for, then who was I?" Slowly, she created a new life for herself, one that included regular visits from her children.

The initial visits were disastrous and Kate came to dread them. Her children were angry at her for abandoning them and Kate was wracked with guilt and despair over not being capable enough to care for her own children. She wanted to be able to provide treats for them, take them to the circus if it was in town, or to see a special play for kids. But she was always on a very tight budget and just managed to make ends meet. A visit from her children always set her back financially and it took her many months to catch up. She became extremely anxious about having her children visit and, increasingly, their times together became very unpleasant. Three years later, Kate's life has become more stable. Her health is better, she has a good job, and she is involved in a new relationship, which gives her much pleasure. She is more able to give of herself to her children; indeed, she has more available to give. In therapy, Kate has worked on understanding her expectations for herself as a mother and her sense of failure about that. She has come to forgive herself for her shortcomings and provide what she can for her children. Her expectations for her visits with her kids have come under scrutiny as well. Her anxiety about these visits has lessened and she and her children are more able to have fun together.

For Kate, as for many other long-distance parents, every time her children come and go is an emotional upheaval in her life. She is reminded once again of the pain of the separation. She is forced to relive the initial letting go, and each subsequent good-bye is a memory of the first. But Kate finds herself less anxious about the whole process; she wouldn't have her children stay away, but she knows that the visits have not been easy times for any of them.

Now I know that we don't have to get all emotionally charged up with each visit. We can have a great time together when I can keep it light. Then when it's time to go we'll cry and that's the way it is.

Kate had expected that the sadness would somehow, mercifully, end someday. I don't believe it will. The sadness of being apart from one's children is always there, ready to be tapped. The loss, the regret, the anguish can come to the fore at any moment. What *can* change is how Kate handles her situation. She has learned to go on with her life, understand what happened to her, grow stronger, and be the best mother she can be to her children.

Warren sees his seven-year-old son Derek two or three times a year. The transitions are very difficult for both of them. Derek is often angry at his father, perhaps for being so far away most of the time. "When I know I'm going to see Derek, I brace myself for a stormy period ahead," says Warren. His outbursts usually last for several days, followed by one good week together—and then it's time to say good-bye. It's not a happy situation for either Warren or Derek, but their relationship is important to both of them and so they continue on in the best way they know how.

Daryl's father lives 150 miles away; sometimes that distance feels as if it might as well be 1,150 miles. They see each other one weekend a month, holidays, and summers. When they first get together, the reunions are always very joyous. "We hug, we kiss, and we laugh a lot," says Daryl, age eight. When Daryl and his dad first had to say good-bye to one another, however, it was very difficult for both of them. It's been four years now since the initial separation and the passing of time has made the separations a bit easier. "My dad always reminds me that he is in my heart and I am in his and that he always loves me. I think about that a lot." His father thinks about that a lot too, and while it doesn't diminish his pain, those thoughts do seem to comfort him.

"I've gone through a lot of crap in my life," says John, "but the hardest thing I've ever done was to put my daughter on the plane after her first visit here." John was so upset after Vanessa left that he cried like a baby. He describes the feeling as being similar to cutting off an arm. "A part of me, something I cared about so deeply, was being forcefully removed. It was devastating to me."

John's account of separating from his daughter is typical for many long-distance parents. They talk of gut-wrenching experiences, feelings of being ripped apart by the separation. The only thing that has eased the pain for these parents has been time. It does get easier as time goes on. As children get older, they are more able to communicate over the phone and can express themselves with greater ease. Relationships between parent and child often become extremely close, and somehow, the distance doesn't seem quite as unbearable.

Christine, whose son Scott lives in England, finds that saying good-bye is always tough, no matter how much she plans for that time in advance. She decided early on in their separation never to tell Scott that she missed him. "If I told him that, he'd wonder why I wouldn't want him to live with me." Christine feels her son is better off living with his father and she doesn't want to do anything to make it more difficult for him. She keeps her sadness to herself and tries to stay upbeat with Scott. Driving to the airport, her heart is very heavy, but the talk is about their next visit together and all the things they'll do when they see each other again.

Lynne on the other hand, makes it a point to tell her son Jonathan, age thirteen, that she misses him "*sooooo* much." She is a long-distance parent to one son who lives in Florida with his dad, while her other son Benjamin, age twelve, lives with her in Vermont. This is not an unusual situation, as I have discovered. Lynne had been having a terrible time parenting both boys. The boys quarreled constantly when they were together and she and her ex-husband decided that the best arrangement for their family would be for each of them to raise one son. Lynne's advice to other long-distance parents is to "KEEP YOUR HEART OPEN!" Both she and her children are sad that there is distance between them, but she also thinks this situation is best for all of them. In other families I spoke with about split custody—that is, one child with one parent and another child with the other—

all spoke of the longing the children felt not only for the other parent but for their other sibling as well.

Paula Rosen, Ph.D., a family therapist specializing in issues of divorce and custody, feels that if the siblings separate when sibling rivalry is most intense, "the children will be deprived of a normal stage of development and an important opportunity to resolve the rivalry and enter into more of a cooperative friendship." The age at which the siblings separate is really the critical factor here. How much time they have had together under the same roof will help determine how closely bonded they are to one another. When siblings are split up at an early age, they lose the sense of family they would have if they grew up together and it is difficult to re-create that.

Anita and her ex-husband have split custody of their two children. It has been a grueling experience for Anita, and one that she shares with candor. "I finally feel normal again, now that my daughter is with me." Anita had been living in Georgia with her husband and two children when she had a nervous breakdown. She came North to be with her family and found work; then she and her husband decided to divorce. "I felt like a mom again in the summers when the kids would come visit me. When they left, it would just kill me." Things got easier for Anita as time went by, although Anita describes herself as a very sad person during the years when neither child was with her. Her daughter had wanted to come live with her for many years, but Anita could not afford the lengthy court battle her ex-husband would have put her through. In the state of Georgia, children can decide where they want to live at age fourteen, so Anita asked her daughter to wait until then. Anita's twelve-year-old son lives in Georgia with his father.

Anita's children lived together for ten years before they were split up. Now, she says, "they fight the same as any other brother and sister, and then they watch out for each other, too." Her son is with her and her daughter for two months during the summer, and there is an adjustment period for all of them. Her daughter is jealous when her brother arrives. Anita's son is very glad to see his sister, as well as his mother, but then becomes angry at his mother, saying that she made a big mistake when she initially left both children in Georgia.

Anita encourages her children to speak to each other weekly during the year. She feels they have a close relationship and both she and her ex-husband make sure that they spend time together at Christmas and on special trips. Anita's son will have the same option her daughter had at age fourteen. He will be able to decide if he wants to remain with his dad or come North to live with his mom. His sister will be off at college by then, probably back in the South. Anita has no idea what he will decide to do. He is able to have more material possessions with his dad than he could have with her and he is angry at her for abandoning him. Yet he is very close to his mother emotionally and they talk very openly together.

Anita becomes very upset when her son accuses her of making a terrible mistake by leaving her children with their father. Anita agrees that she did make a mistake and says that she can't undo what's been done. "I can't take back the years," says Anita, "and it still makes me very upset." Finding a support group for mothers without custody helped ease Anita's pain. She met other women whose young children lived far away. She finally felt as if she wasn't all alone. "The group turned the key for me. You can get so down on yourself for abandoning your children. The group helped me work through the guilt."

To find a support group in your community, you may have to do some detective work. First, see if there is a chapter of Parents Without Partners. This is a national organization that provides emotional and social support to single parents. They may know of a specific group dealing with long-distance parents. Next, call your local family service agency or your local mental health association. They might either run such a support group themselves or steer you in the right direction. Mothers Without Custody is another national organization that has chapters around the country. You can write them at P.O. Box 56762, Houston, Texas 77256 and request information regarding a support group near you. Fathers and Children's Equality (FACE) is an organization that supports men in their desire to be active fathers. There might be a chapter in your area in which other long-distance fathers participate. Should all these efforts fail, start your own group. Put an ad in your local newspaper, saying "Long-distance parent wishes to form support group with others in similar situation." You will definitely have to expend some energy, but the rewards of sharing experiences with others will be well worth it.

When they say good-bye to their children, some long-distance parents know that they won't be seeing them again for a very long time. Others live very far away from their children and the good-byes seem that much more poignant. Irwin and his daughter Naomi, age eight, see each other once a year. Finances prohibit any more visiting than that. When they first get together, Irwin makes it a point to ease any initial awkwardness between them as best he can. "I try to make it seem as if we never parted. I scoop her up in my arms and hug her a lot. She always responds warmly to me, too."

"Go slow, give it time to settle," says Cliff, a long-distance parent to his seven-year-old daughter Isabelle, who lives in Holland with her mother. Cliff sees his daughter two or three times a year, which he has been doing since she was two years old. They talk on the phone about once a month and Cliff sends her lots of cards and letters. Cliff has learned that it takes Isabelle time to get to know him with each visit. He has become more cautious when he and his daughter first reunite. He takes his cues from her and waits for her to become comfortable with him. "My relationship with my daughter is an integral part of my life, even though we live so far apart."

The most difficult aspect of being a long-distance parent for Cliff is the separation after the visits. He feels terrible when he has to leave Isabelle, and the intensity of the feeling stays with him for many weeks. It is difficult for him to resume his normal routine back in the States, and he finds himself yearning to be with his daughter. He knows that at least four or five months will pass before he sees her again, and this makes the separation all that more painful. Cliff's ex-wife tells him that Isabelle also has a terrible time after he leaves. She goes through her own period of readjustment and acts out a lot of her anger and frustration with her mother. This makes Cliff feel even worse for having left his daughter.

Rick talks about how heartbroken he used to feel when he'd say good-bye to his son. He'd have no energy for weeks and would keep running a mental videotape in his head of what he didn't have in his life—his son. Now when it's time to say good-bye, he keeps a vision in his head of his own life back home. Rick says this makes the good-byes just a little bit easier for him.

> I used to have severe aftershocks after a visit with my son. Now when it's time to go home, I just go and get back to work.

What is it like for the parent whose children board the plane for two weeks with their long-distance parent? If you are the local parent, then you, too, experience a whole range of emotions when your children leave for extended visits with your ex-partner. You may feel relieved that you are finally getting a long-deserved break from twenty-four-hour-a-day child-care responsibilities. You may feel angry that your ex-partner has it easy, with full-time responsibility for the kids for only two weeks every four months or so. Perhaps you feel very sad and lonely as you watch your children board the plane. What will you do without them around? Your life may feel very empty without them and you may miss them terribly.

In an article that appeared in the *Philadelphia Inquirer,* a custodial parent, H. G. Bissinger, described how he felt putting his five-year-old twin boys on the plane to visit their mother in California at Christmas

time. His life is so intertwined with theirs, he is so involved in their every activity, that not to have them at
home leaves him with a feeling of tremendous loss. The
night before the boys are to leave, there are endless hugs
and kisses and "I love yous" shared. One of the boys
asks his dad not to cry when he leaves because he'll be
back. At the airport, as the boys board the plane, they
are very excited and their father is very sad. "I do not
cry, because I have promised. And all I can feel is a
stunning silence, the silence of being alone, the silence
of being without my children."

Many local parents use the time their children are
away to discover what they themselves really enjoy doing. One mother I know had a fantasy of crawling into
bed after work each day when her kids were gone and
reading good books. She did that on the first day, and
then felt the quiet overwhelm her. All she could think of
was the kids—were they all right? Did they miss her? The
next night, she went to an aerobics class. On the third
night, she was back in bed with her good books (and
aching body) and made that part of her routine until her
children returned. Although the quiet scared her at first,
she was later able to enjoy the peace that the time spent
alone brought her.

When children visit their long-distance parent for an
entire summer, or a good part of it, the loss for the local
parent is even more acute. It can be difficult to establish
a new routine that is centered wholly on oneself. There
is no need to rush home after work and cook dinner for
the kids. If you have remarried and now are child-free,
this is a special time for you and your partner to spend
some time together alone (providing that his children
from a former marriage aren't coming to visit).

Whether you are the local or the long-distance parent, the way you handle separations in your life, in general, will be a good indicator of how you will handle the
separation from your children. Separations are a re-
minder of earlier times in our lives, times we may not
even be conscious of. Issues around separation are so

fundamental to who we are as people that when children leave home, it triggers our own sense of loss, of being abandoned as children. That abandonment might have come in the form of a parent who died, or a parent who was dysfunctional in some way (due to alcoholism, or a health problem, perhaps), who was not able to care for you properly. Or perhaps you were the fourth child in a family of seven children, and your mother simply did not have the time to love you in the deep, emotional way that children need. You will then live your life as an adult with a feeling of loss, feeling that you didn't get what you needed on a psychological level.

Nor need there be such drama. For the great majority of us, the issue of loss is universal. All of us can relate to a time in our lives when a loved one left us, either through ending a relationship prematurely, by divorce or death, or simply going away on an extended trip. We can also remember times when a loved one threatened to leave, which might have left us in a state of panic. When we are aware of our feelings, it is common that the feeling of abandonment, of being left, surfaces. This sense of loss naturally gets transferred to a situation in which your child is away from you. Some parents have a very difficult time when their children visit their other parent, even for as little as two weeks. For the long-distance parent, the separation from a child can be debilitating for long periods of time.

A compassionate partner who can comfort you and hold you when the tears come helps to ease the pain for that moment, but the sorrow will recur. A network of caring friends and family who listen to your distress can be a source of comfort to you; it always helps if you are not alone. But pain is pain. When you lose somebody, you feel pain. This is a normal experience when your child leaves you, whether it's for two weeks or four months.

Time often diminishes the intensity of the emotion. Many parents report that they didn't think they could ever live through the initial separation from their children.

There was nothing else in their lives to fill the void previously occupied by the child's presence. And yet, somehow, the acute pain subsided and they were able to go on
with their lives.

Sometimes, only a professional can help ease the se-
vere pain that a parent experiences when a child leaves
home. In my work with clients, I ask them to recall other
painful times when they have experienced deep loss and
how they handled those times. I comfort them, listen to
their grief, and validate the reality of their feelings. Of
course, they feel terrible and have every right to feel that
way. I help them see that it is not because they are weak
or needy that they have such deep pain over a child being
away from them. Rather, it is because they allow themselves to experience the fragility of the human condition,
as well as the deep bond that exists between them and
their child, that they are able to feel the anguish of being
apart from a loved one. Pain is a healthy and normal
response to these circumstances. People can't rise above
it until they allow themselves to experience it in all its
misery. Time really is the great healer.

There is no set time limit in which you'll feel better.
Some people read a book quickly; others take years to
finish. When divorce first became prevalent, mental
health professionals said that it took people one year to
complete the mourning process. Now, years and many
many divorces later, we are learning that some people
begin building new lives almost immediately and others
may take a much longer time, even three to five years.
One way is no more normal than the next.

To help people move on with their lives, I ask them
to think about the ways in which their child being away
could be an opportunity for them. Perhaps they have been
centered on their child for a long time and have not attended to developing parts of themselves. I had been divorced for ten years and then remarried at the same time
my son left home. Although I resisted seeing his leaving
home as an opportunity, his absence did give me the time
to devote to building my new family with my husband

and stepdaughter. It was also a time in which my work flourished. Looking back on that time, I see that my absorption in my work and the great gusto with which I took it on was a way for me to assuage my grief over losing my son. With time, I was also able to see that my relationship with Josh deepened with the separation from him. Our conversations were richer and more intimate and the time we spent together was extraordinarily special for both of us. That remains so to this day.

Reunions and good-byes are the symbol of the best and worst aspects of being a long-distance parent. Everyone goes through the excitement of a reunion and the despondency of a good-bye. There don't seem to be any shortcuts to make the process easier. The nagging questions and worries you had at the beginning of the separation may reappear with recurring separations. Did you do the right thing? Is this the best place for your child to be? The guilt long-distance parents feel lingers on and surfaces at the worst times. But the joy of reuniting with our long-distance children makes everything worthwhile. The worst of times will pass, and the pleasure of deep and lasting relationships with our children, across the miles, will increase.

CHAPTER 7

Remarriage and the Long-Distance Family

Remarriage. For a long-distance parent away from his child, the very word conjures up images of being odd man out. Your ex-wife is remarrying. A man you don't even know will be spending more time with your children than you do. Maybe this man will replace you as their father. Maybe they'll start to call him Dad. Maybe the kids won't want to come visit you anymore, since they will have a more normal family life now. They probably won't call you as much since they'll have another man to go to for fatherly advice. Maybe your ex-wife won't call you as much to talk about the kids, since she'll have a new husband to do that with now.

If you are a long-distance mother and your ex-husband remarries, you probably think your children may be better off with a female influence in the home, but they also might need you less. Now someone else will be raising your children. If you had any hope of your children returning to live with you, the reality of their father remarrying might change all that. The children might prefer to remain in a two-parent home; the courts may also feel this would be best.

When their ex-husbands remarry, long-distance mothers often don't know who the parent in charge is. The father might relinquish many of his parenting responsibilities to his new partner, thus putting the stepmother in charge of arranging schedules and seeing to the children's basic needs. The long-distance mother then is forced to deal with the stepmother, whom she might not know at all. She feels awkward and uncomfortable in this new role. Her status as a mother is even more reduced.

When an ex-partner remarries, all kinds of worries crop up. Even if you yourself have already remarried, your concerns about how your ex's new marriage will affect you, your children, and your long-distance relationship with them are legitimate concerns. You may worry about whether the new partner will support and encourage your contacts with your children. Maybe he'll want to put a stop to the driving that your ex-wife has always been willing to do, in order to meet you halfway on the road when you get the kids. Maybe he'll want the schedule changed altogether. Or maybe he won't have anything at all to say about it. It's just that you don't know, and not knowing who this man is, never mind how he feels about you and your children, leaves you feeling very anxious indeed.

If you have a fairly good relationship with your ex-partner, you can begin to resolve some of this anxiety by talking about your concerns. Tell your ex that you don't want anything to change with the children. Then tell her that you realize things will change and that you will do your best to be flexible and to work things out with her. You do want to be considered in the new plans and to be informed of any changes ahead of time. Tell her that you are still and always will be the kids' father, that you don't want them taking anyone else's name, and that you don't want them to call him Dad.

If you don't have a fairly good relationship with your ex-partner, begin to talk about some of your concerns anyway. Write your ex a letter if you are uncomfortable speaking with her on the phone. Tell her you are pleased for her that she found someone new (are you?) and that you wish her every happiness (do you?). Then go on to tell her that you hope she will continue to do everything possible to assist you in maintaining your long-distance relationship with your children. You, in turn, will continue paying child support!

It is in your best interest to develop civil relationships with your ex-partner and the new spouse. Even if you are not particularly fond of your ex, you may surprise yourself to discover that you actually like their new mate. The calming influence of the new partner may be reflected in your relationship with your ex-partner. It might be easier for you to make arrangements concerning the children, either with your ex-spouse or with the new mate.

It's a mistake to assume that things will get worse because your ex-partner remarries. Things might improve, both in your relationship with your children and with your ex-mate. Your ex might be more interested in the children visiting you for longer periods of time so he can be alone with his new wife. Or your children, too, might welcome more time away from new people in the house—a stepmother and possibly stepsiblings as well.

All the emotions you felt when you first divorced or when you first became a long-distance parent are likely to resurface when your ex-partner remarries. You may feel lonely, guilty, powerless, hurt, disenfranchised, upset, angry, or depressed. The range of emotions you may experience at this time may not seem rational to you. After all, your divorce took place years ago. Why be upset over a remarriage now?

The initial feelings of loss at the time your marriage broke up will probably reappear to trouble you at this time. Feelings of longing for your ex-partner may re-emerge when she remarries. The distance between you and your children at this time heightens your sense of being alone and apart from the rest of the family. Evan, a long-distance father of three girls, put it this way: ''The day my ex-wife told me she was going to remarry, I felt so left out. We had been divorced and living far apart from each other for years, but at that moment, I wished our family had never come apart and that we were all together again.''

"Guilt is the gift that keeps on giving," says popular columnist Erma Bombeck. Long-distance parents know this better than anybody. When you are far away from the children and your ex is about to remarry, feelings of guilt and remorse soar. If only you lived closer to the children, you would be able to have more of an impact on their lives, even if they have a new stepmother. They would know, for sure, that you are their mother and they wouldn't have any confusion about who to call Mom. If only you had spent more time with them when they were younger. Maybe they'd want to come live with you at this point in their lives. At least the oldest one, anyway.

Up until the point of remarriage, many long-distance parents feel that although they don't exercise a lot of control over their children's lives, their ex-partner, someone they originally chose to be the other parent for their children, runs the show. For many long-distance parents, this somehow makes it easier to relinquish control. With the arrival of a new partner on the scene, long-distance parents experience loss of control at a deeper level. "A stranger will be telling my kids what to do," says Evan. "What if I don't like his values? I guess that's too bad for me, and too bad for my kids."

The strong feelings that accompany the news of a remarriage will probably subside with time. Long-distance parents need to make adjustments in the way they relate to their children and to their ex-mate. Often, there is a tendency on the part of the long-distance parent to pull back from the children after a remarriage. Some of this may be self-protective, as the parent feels that the children are going to be doing this themselves. Long-distance parents may call less often, not wanting to intrude on what they assume is now one big happy family. They often shut themselves out first, before they are told to call less often.

But you don't have to do it! Don't withdraw from your children at a time when they have a strong need to be close to you. They need the continuity in their lives that their relationship with you provides. They need to know that you will always be their parent, no matter what. You can be a buffer for them, someone to talk to who is outside their home. Long-distance parents might hear news of the new stepparent that could be disturbing, whether favorable or unfavorable. It's important to remember to let your children know that you want to hear about everything in their lives, including news about their new stepfamily. However many feelings you have about the new family constellation, your children are going through their own adjustment to living with a new parent and possibly new stepsiblings. Take a deep breath, and no matter how painful it might be for you, be a good parent to your children. Listen to what they have to say about the changes taking place in their family life and see how you can support them in making the situation a good one.

After things settle down and you sense some changes have been made in their schedule, ask them when would be a good time to call. Sunday morning still may be best, but they may have a family breakfast now, or go to church on Sunday morning. Ask your ex-partner if there are any changes you should know about that would interfere with the routine you have established with your children for staying in touch. Don't assume that everything will remain the same. It probably won't.

State very clearly to your ex-partner that although she has remarried, you want very much to remain active concerning the children. You want to be involved in decision-making and you want to be informed of any special or unusual circumstances. Most long-distance parents are able to maintain their relationships with their children after remarriage takes place. They are not shut out of decision-making concerning their children, although they are probably consulted less frequently. If you are the parent remarrying, Robert E. Adler, Ph.D., author of *Sharing the Children,* suggests that you "make every effort to include the children's other parent in their lives. Children adjust better to remarriage when they have secure, positive relationships with both of their parents."

If you as the long-distance parent remarry, you will want to give your children and ex-partner time to adjust to the news before the event actually happens. I hope your children will have met their new stepparent and have established a friendly relationship. Include your children as much as possible in planning for your new life. You need to reassure your children that although you are re-marrying and will have stepchildren and possibly children of your own, their interests and needs will always be of primary concern to you. They probably won't believe you and words alone will not convince them. It will be your actions and behavior that will tell them whether you really mean what you say.

The more people there are in any family constellation, the more complicated life is. For the long-distance parent, a new partner, stepchildren, and possible additional children of your own means that there will be more feelings to contend with, more people's needs to take into account, and more schedules to accommodate. It is not at all unlikely that this might be marriage number three for you, leaving behind other children and relationships unattended.

Consider the following: Lila and Ron were married and had two children, Craig and Maggie. Lila and Ron subsequently divorced, and in order to pursue a more lucrative career, Ron moved five hundred miles away from his children. They saw him regularly, on all holidays and during the summer. Ron then married Kristen, a woman who had a daughter, Heidi, presently living with her. Ron became very attached to Heidi and thought of her as his own child. Heidi's father lived in the same town and saw his daughter from time to time. Ron and Kristen had two other children of their new union.

And Lila? She, too, remarried. Her husband Gary did not get along well with Craig and Maggie and wanted Lila all to himself. His happiest times where when Lila's kids went to visit their father. In fact, he was overjoyed when Craig announced that he wanted to go live with his father full time. Lila, however, did not share his joy. She felt there were too many kids already in Ron's household and Craig wouldn't get the attention he needed.

Lila was always juggling her husband's need to be alone with her and the needs of her children, also to be alone with her. There was never enough of her to go around. Lila's inclination was to let Craig go live with his father. At least that would mean one less child for Gary to get angry with and one less distraction for her. "I feel like I'm being torn apart," said Lila. The unspoken jealousy and competition for her affection were about to ruin her second marriage. It was Gary who suggested they go for family counseling. He did not want to lose his wife. They talked about all their unrealized dreams and sense of failure and wondered if they could salvage their relationship. They had so many people's needs to consider that they lost track of their own.

What Lila and Gary learned in counseling was that they would both have to do a lot of compromising in order to save their marriage. Lila would have to be less protective of her children and allow them more independence, and Gary would have to include them more in his life. When Gary was nice to her children, Lila was grateful and loved him more. In time, Craig did go live with his father. But he went not because he was unhappy with his mother and stepfather, but because he felt close to his father and wanted to spend more time with him. Gary felt as if he became the long-distance father. He kept in touch with Craig, whose visits back home were pleasant times for everyone.

A simpler scenario is this: Annette and Mario divorce, their teenage daughter Alexandra lives with her mother and visits her father often. Annette then marries Sal, whose son Tony lives with his mother. During the summers, they play musical children. Alexandra visits her father, and Tony comes to stay with Annette and Sal. Annette and Sal are never without children. During the Christmas holidays, Alexandra is away with her father and Tony is present with his father and Annette. There is always a stepparent, stepchild situation. Tensions rise and fall, depending on people's moods, and although they do the best they can, it is rarely smooth sailing at Annette and Sal's house. Annette would like to have a week's vacation with her husband, with no children, but in their five years of marriage, that has yet to happen.

It is unlikely that this will happen unless Annette becomes a more assertive and creative woman. She is in a difficult position, because a vacation alone would mean Sal's son not coming to visit. She would not be sacrificing any time with her own daughter. Tony is in school, so he couldn't visit just as easily at another time. What would be possible, however, is Sal going to visit Tony on his home ground at a different time. This would mean more contact with his ex-wife than he has had for years, which would make him feel very uneasy. Another option is that Alexandra, Annette's daughter, could stay with her aunt and uncle for a week at another time, so Annette and Sal could go off together. Or perhaps Alexandra's father could come and stay with her. All too often, when long-distance relationships are involved, people feel locked into schedules that they feel they can't break. But schedules can be changed and other solutions can be found—if there is a strong desire on the part of the remarried couple to affirm the importance of their own relationship.

Simone married a man who had two children by a previous marriage. The children lived with their mother in a distant town and so Simone considered herself a long-distance stepparent. It was she who maintained the relationship with her stepchildren and encouraged her husband to keep in touch with them. Simone and her husband had two sons of their own and then divorced. She and her sons moved away to a town close to her stepchildren, thus making her ex-husband a long-distance parent with the second set of children as well. Her ex-husband was supposed to move near her and the children but has never done so. Simone is now in an intimate relationship with a man who has two long-distance children living three thousand miles away.

How to keep track of all the relationships in this family constellation? Simone is the central figure. Her ex-husband's first wife told Simone that she was the parent who was committed to her two children, not their father, since it was Simone who kept in touch across the miles. Simone has a close relationship with her stepchildren to this day. Simone's ex-husband has not kept in close touch with his second set of children either. There were years when he missed calling on birthdays and holidays, although he has always sent support payments on time. He has recently remarried and Simone, who has adopted a spiritual approach of accepting life's changes, decided to have a ceremony with her children to mark the event.

> I have validated my children's anger, yet encouraged forgiveness and an open heart. I'd like to teach my children to accept what life offers them—including a limited relationship with their father.

Simone is attempting to make some peace with the chaotic years of long-distance parenting involving numerous children, relationships, and marriages.

One long-distance father sought out my services for his nine-year-old son, who lived with his mother in my community. The father, Chad, and his second wife, Yolanda, lived two and a half hours away. The boy's mother, Janine, was told by the school counselor that her son, Aaron, was having difficulty keeping up with his work, although he was above average intelligence. She was also told that the school counselor considered Aaron to be depressed and recommended that the family seek professional help. Chad didn't believe his ex-wife would follow through on this recommendation. She, too, had remarried, to a man who had custody of a boy Aaron's age, and they had three more children of their own. Chad described Janine as a woman who thought of herself as a good mother, but she was inconsistent and wanted to keep Aaron dependent on her. They had what they considered a civil divorce, and in order to keep it civil, never got into any real dialogue concerning Aaron. Even though he lived 150 miles away, Chad was prepared to come to counseling once a week to help his son.

Yolanda, for her part, was a long-distance stepparent. She saw Aaron every other weekend and for extended periods over the summer. It was only during the summer that Yolanda felt she really got to know Aaron. At first, because her relationship with her own husband was new, there was a lot of competition for Chad's attention. Aaron behaved like a brat at times and Chad did little to help Yolanda and Aaron build a solid relationship.

I felt all alone at first. I wanted Chad to be more understanding, to help Aaron accept me. Chad was very defensive. We were all tugging at each other. It took a whole lot of talking for Chad to see that he did need to have a stronger role in helping us all work things out. He was Aaron's father, after all.

In my work with this family, Chad and Janine have come to see that their divorce wasn't as civil as they had thought. They hadn't really talked to each other since they separated shortly after Aaron's birth. Now they had to realize that Aaron's depression and inability to do his schoolwork were signs that things were not working well at all in this family. Communication had virtually stopped between parents, each of them had remarried within a short period of each other, and Aaron was the spokesperson for the existing conflict in this family.

In all families, whether they are divorced, intact, or remarried, children will act out this unresolved conflict when the spouses or ex-spouses don't deal effectively with their marital and postmarital problems. They might have difficulty with schoolwork, have behavior problems, become depressed or addicted to drugs or alcohol, have trouble with peers. In some way, children will alert their parents to the fact that things are not all right. In this family, Aaron was speaking up loud and clear.

Yolanda was not very excited about the prospects of Chad and Janine being in counseling together. She felt threatened and excluded and wondered where she fit in. She and Janine have had little contact over the four years that she's known Chad, and Yolanda prefers to keep it that way. She feels Janine has been rude and insensitive to her and she prefers to let Chad do all the talking with his ex-wife.

At first, Yolanda thought that she had the raw end of the parenting deal. Janine was number one in Aaron's eyes, Chad was number two, and she came in a sorry number three. Recently, things have turned around a bit. Now that Aaron is better able to express his anger at his parents, he can turn to Yolanda as the neutral third person in his life. Yolanda has worked hard at building her relationship with Aaron over the years and now it is beginning to pay off. He trusts her and feels he can come to her with his problems. This means everything to Yolanda. Because of an infertility problem, she is unable to have children of her own. Her relationship with Aaron helps to alleviate the sadness she feels whenever she thinks about her own loss.

This long-distance family is coming a bit closer together in all its parts. Hopefully, Aaron's parents and stepparents will work more effectively to provide him with the emotional support he needs to find his place among all the people in his life. Within a short time after counseling began, Aaron's teacher reported a marked improvement in his schoolwork. His depression is slowly lifting and he is pleased to know that his parents are talking to each other about him.

Whether you are the custodial or the long-distance parent, you open yourself up to another person's opinion about how your child should be raised when you remarry. This is the most delicate issue for remarried partners to face. There is no one more wrathful than a parent scorned. You are at your most vulnerable. Your new partner's criticism of your child, or how you are raising your child, feels like a slap in the face. The natural parent gets defensive ("Well, *you're* not doing such a hot job yourself!"), and instead of feeling as if you have a friend, your new mate takes on all the characteristics of an enemy. Somehow, you feel that the new mate has no right to criticize your child, even if the criticism is valid. Different values become evident and differences in child-rearing practices erupt very dramatically. When your child is six hundred miles away and having a tough time, you do not want to be told by your new mate that you are being too soft on the boy.

Actually, what you do want to be told by your mate is very little. You want your mate to listen to your concerns about your child, to help you clarify your own position, and to make suggestions or give advice only if you ask for it. And then if you ask for advice, you want it understood that your obligation is to listen to it, not necessarily to follow it.

Distance creates dissonance. If you constantly tell your present partner how awful your ex-spouse is, you won't be able to get objective advice about how to communicate effectively with your ex. You've polluted the atmosphere; your present spouse can only be negative about your ex-spouse, since that's all you've ever said. Your current spouse may not want to criticize your ex, feeling that might mean criticism of you, since you married that person and were in love when you did so. When there are long distances involved, your current and ex-spouse don't usually meet at all, and if they do, it's very sporadic.

If you are remarried and either or both of you has a long-distance child, you are very well aware of the unique sets of problems this situation poses. Christmas is coming. Your son is going to visit his long-distance dad, and your present husband's daughter is coming to visit you. Your son is never with you at Christmastime, while your stepdaughter always is. Somehow this doesn't seem fair to you.

"Parents who celebrate holidays and special occasions with their stepchildren when their own children are off visiting their other natural parent often resent the situation," says Cherie Burns, author of *Stepmotherhood, How to Survive Without Feeling Frustrated, Left Out or Wicked.* Burns recommends that stepparents give up the notion that everyone has to be together at holiday time. She suggests that a more relaxed time is found when everyone in the family can be together, thus eliminating some of the high expectations and deep feelings that usually surround family gatherings at holidays.

If you do get together on holidays, talk with every family member about holiday traditions. Explain to your new partner exactly what about the holiday is important to you. Ask the children how they would like to celebrate. Traditional dishes take on great significance when they're unexpectedly not part of the dinner menu. Is there an old family tradition that you would like to bring to your new family? When are the presents opened? When do you attend synagogue or church services? As in all stepfamily relations, it is best not to assume that you all do it the same way, whatever *it* is.

However you plan to celebrate, the outcome will be most satisfying if you keep your expectations to a minimum. The Norman Rockwell holiday family will probably not be gathering in your newly remarried home. You can count on feelings of divided loyalties cropping up. Long-distance children who are with you for the holidays will naturally miss their parent back home. Encourage them to call and stay in touch; remind them that they don't have to choose one parent over the other. Tell them you understand how they must feel at a special time like this, wanting to be with both parents and knowing they can't.

Vacations often pose problems for long-distance families. As a long-distance parent with a finite number of weeks for vacations, you have to decide if you will spend all of this time with your long-distance child, or if you will divide up some of the time to spend with your

new family. There are tugs in all directions. Your new
spouse may be willing to fly to Chicago to see little
Jimmy for part of her vacation time, but certainly not all
of it. You, on the other hand, want to get in all the time
you can with your son. You can be with your spouse any
time, but you've always saved vacation time for Jimmy.
Or perhaps your new stepchildren aren't interested in going backpacking—the kind of vacation you and Jimmy
enjoy most. Just walking in the woods, fishing in a
mountain stream, cooking out—that's heaven for you and
your boy. Her children think two weeks lying on the
beach is more like it.

Several case scenarios illustrate the need for talking
over vacation plans to avoid feelings of resentment on the
part of some family member or other.

• Nick and his family spent a few very miserable
vacations together. Now they've decided to split up the
time. His wife takes her kids to the beach for a week
while Nick goes off to the woods with Jimmy. Then Nick
and Jimmy join them at the beach for another week, and
they're all glad to see each other. "It's really very simple," says Nick. "We are not one big happy family, and
as soon as we stopped pretending that we were, things
were much better for everyone."

• Carla and her second husband, Donald, wanted to
take a week's vacation alone, without her long-distance
son and without his in-house daughter, who would be
visiting with her long-distance mom. When Carla's son
heard about the plans, he just assumed he'd be invited to
come along, or at least to join them for a few days, since
he hadn't seen his mom in quite some time and the vacation spot was near his home. Carla felt pulled. She
wanted to see her son and she wanted much-needed time
alone with her husband. Donald didn't feel pulled at all.
He didn't want her son along for any amount of time on
this trip. Carla finally told her son that this trip was not
going to include him, but she did invite him to come visit
for a week later in the summer. She would take some

time off from work, and they'd do the things just they loved to do together. Donald's daughter would still be away, Donald would be able to spend some time with Carla's son, which he enjoyed doing, and Carla wouldn't be trying to please the various factions of her family. She'd be able to devote herself to her son, which to Carla was a rare and wonderful thing.

There are many ways to work out family vacations, even though the circumstances look very difficult to manage. The key here is to tell the truth about how you really want it to be for yourself and your partner, and go from there. It might be hard to tell your second husband that you have no interest in spending your hard-earned vacation time with his children. But you have no basis for negotiating any other kind of vacation unless you voice your true feelings. You could of course choose not to say anything and be miserable the whole time, wishing you were somewhere else. But that's not being kind to yourself or to the other members of your family. In your desire to find new solutions to situations that historically have caused hurt feelings in your family, be creative. You and your partner have come up with options one and two. Don't stop there. What would option number three be? Is there an alternative that you haven't even considered yet? Just because "it's always been that way" doesn't mean that you are locked in to spending vacations "that way" for the rest of your child-raising years. Use your friends and family members to help you brainstorm.

Original Family:
Lance, the husband
Anne, the wife
Patrick, age 25
Randy, age 22
Lauren, age 13

Remarried Family:
Lou, the husband
Anne, the wife
Sean, age 16 (Lou's son who lives with him)
Beverly, age 14 (lives with her mother, in and out of her father's home)
Lauren, age 13

Lance remembers the day his ex-wife Anne told him she was moving to Kansas to remarry and would take Lauren, who was then nine, with her. He was very angry about it at the time, although he didn't try to stop her in any way. "She was just picking up my daughter and moving away," says Lance. Anne was marrying Lou, a man who was an old friend of the family's. Knowing who Lou was and that he was a decent human being made the decision an easier one for Lance to accept. He knew that Lauren would be well cared for by Lou. What he didn't know was how difficult it would be for Lauren to adjust to a new geography, a new culture, and a new family. Sean, Lou's son, was vicious to Lauren, and made her life miserable on a daily basis. Lauren would call her father and cry about how unhappy she was. Lance felt there was little he could do to ease the situation for Lauren. He would talk to Anne and Anne would talk to Lou and still Sean was nasty. In addition, Lou's daughter Beverly, age fourteen, lived with her mother in a nearby community and was in and out of Lou's home as an honored guest. This added to the confusion for Lauren who felt she had no place in her new home.

Lauren had some other problems to deal with. Lance was gay; Lauren had known this since the time her parents had separated, when she was four years old. Understandably, it was easier for her to handle this when she lived in a large East Coast city. In small-town Kansas, she kept this piece of information to herself, thus feeling even more isolated. In the last year, Lauren told her two friends that her dad was gay—her best friend, and another girl whose father was also gay. Lauren recently told her dad that it was okay that he was gay, but "I worry about you getting AIDS."

Lance has just been diagnosed as having AIDS. He called Anne, told her the news, and asked her to tell Lauren. He would follow up with a phone call. When he called Lauren to discuss it with her, they cried on the phone together. "AIDS meant death to her as well as to me. I wanted her to come and see I was alive." At

Lance's request, Anne and Lauren flew to New York to see him in the hospital. Lance and Anne's two older sons were also present, so it was a bittersweet reunion of the original family.

In the nine years since they have been divorced, Lance and Anne have always been reasonable with each other. They have worked out most of their differences amicably. Having known him for many years, Lance has felt a sense of kinship with Anne's new husband. In this time of crisis, Lance and Anne together have been able to provide support for their three children. Lance has worked hard to maintain a close relationship with his daughter and Anne has helped him in this. Lauren has always wanted her father to come visit her in Kansas. She wants him to see her life there, meet her friends, spend a day in school with her. Over the years, Lance has resisted doing this. He's always felt it would be too painful to actually see how much he misses out on. "I haven't figured out yet how to go to Kansas emotionally," says Lance, "but I don't have much longer to wait." He plans to take a trip there this fall.

Even when relations among the ex-spouses and remarried families are fairly smooth, it is difficult to have two worlds merge. Some people prefer to keep things very separate, for the reason that Lance mentioned. It is just too painful to be physically in the place where your child lives and to experience firsthand how much of your child's life you are missing.

I spoke earlier of a visit I made to Vermont to see Josh in a school play. I was struck by how lonely I felt in that audience, sitting next to my ex-husband's new wife. She knew all of Josh's friends and their parents. She knew who Josh had a crush on and whose house the cast party would be at. She was privy to all the important gossip about Josh's life. While I had met some of his friends, we never had an extended conversation together. I certainly had never talked to any of his friends' parents. I was one out-of-it long-distance parent, feeling very much an outsider listening to Josh's stepmother tell me about his life. What an awful feeling! Still, it was better to go to Vermont than it would have been not to, and I suspect that Lance will feel the same way after his visit to Kansas. On a positive note, after that visit I was more able to converse with Josh about his friends and had seen faces to go along with names I had heard. And in the end, I felt less of an outsider for having been there.

One of the ways long-distance children feel excluded is that they are often not present at family gatherings. They feel left out of the larger family because they're not present at most family events. Relatives really don't know them that well. Long-distance parents, too, often feel isolated and sad at family gatherings because their own children are far away. While long-distance children might maintain some relationship with their grandparents, they are unlikely to stay in touch with assorted aunts and uncles and cousins. Vacations are a good time for family reunions, for your long-distance child to see his relatives and to be seen by them.

> It makes me sad that my son doesn't see my own parents that much. I'm in North Carolina, my son is in Texas, and my parents are in California. It's hard to get everyone together.—Billy

Two years ago, Billy and his son drove out to California to visit his parents. Billy, like many long-distance parents, only takes vacations when he can be with his son. He doesn't go on separate vacations with his second wife. He gets two weeks off a year and his priority is to be with his son. If his wife wants to come along, that's fine, but the time is clearly intended for Billy and his son. If they don't go to visit his parents, then they travel to visit one of Billy's brothers or sister. Billy feels strongly that he wants his son to know his own family, and the only way he knows how to do this is to use his vacation time for family visits.

While this arrangement may be satisfying for Billy, his second wife resents the lack of vacation time alone with him and is less willing to be accommodating. This couple will have to work out alternative solutions in order for their relationship to flourish.

It can be difficult to keep up extended family relations when your children live far away and when their other parent has remarried. Often, then, the children become involved in their new family life; their stepparents' parents become their more active grandparents, especially if they all live in the same community. Some children have as many as four sets of grandparents! Stepgrandparents, however, would probably not be as interested in their stepgrandchildren as would grandparents by birth. While these new relationships take on some meaning for your long-distance children, their real grandparents, your parents, are the ones to whom they have a deeper connection.

As in your own long-distance relationship with your children, continuity is an important factor for grandparents and their grandchildren. Wallerstein and Kelly, in *Surviving the Breakup*, noted that children of divorce "who had extended families, especially grandparents, who were close by or who kept up a continuing interest from a distance, were very much helped by this support system." Grandparents can often be a stabilizing force in the life of a child whose parents have divorced. They can offer constancy, unconditional love, and a sense of security for children. Parents may divorce, but grandparents don't divorce their grandchildren. Some grandparents, however, withdraw from their grandchildren after a divorce. They don't know what their role is in the divorced family, especially if there is conflict between them and their own children. They don't know how to relate to their grandchildren, may not want to get caught in the middle between ex-spouses, and don't know what their rights are, if any. Greif and Pabst, in *Mothers Without Custody*, feel that another layer of complexity is added to family dynamics when grandparents are involved with their grandchildren after a divorce. "In ideal situations, grandparents provide the children with a supportive and stable relationship that is not affected by their parents' conflict. In less ideal situations, grandparents may be pulled into taking sides.''

Across the country, grandparents have become involved in lobbying efforts to ensure their right to visit with their grandchildren after divorce, no matter who gets custody. Grandparents visitation laws have been enacted in many states. In a note in the *Columbia Law Review* in January, 1986 ("The Constitutional Constraints on Grandparents' Visitation Statutes"), the authors state, "In the last two decades, there has been a strong movement to create a legal right for grandparents to visit their grandchildren. Since 1965, forty-eight states have enacted legislation giving grandparents a statutory right to petition for court-enforced visitation, forty-one of these since 1975.''

Many grandparents do not want to be shut out of their grandchildren's lives. They don't want to lose out on the unique relationship available to them with their grandchildren. In an interview I conducted with my mother, she said that when she heard the news that Josh was moving with his father to Vermont, "I felt rotten. I was afraid I wouldn't see him often and that I'd lose touch with him.'' Over the years, Josh has maintained contact with my parents, but instead of seeing them as often as he used to, visits are now sparse. Occasionally, there is direct contact between them in letters and phone calls, but mostly the connection is through me. I keep my parents informed about news of Josh. What makes it easier for my parents is to know that his father is doing a very good job with Josh and that we all are in constant touch. "I was glad, too, that Josh had an opportunity to live in a different part of the country," said my mother. "The experience has been good for him.''

To keep your long-distance children connected to their grandparents, examine your own relationship with your parents. You may feel resentful if you see your own parents giving love and affection to your children in a way they never did with you. You may be angry at your parents and feel your children would be better off without them. If your parents want to have a relationship with their grandchildren, would you stand in the way? Your children may need them now, more than ever. Don't allow your differences with your parents to interfere with the important role they can play in your children's lives.

A civil relationship with your ex-partner will make it easier for you to ask him to assist you in maintaining extended family relations for your child. Many local parents I interviewed keep in touch regularly with their ex-in-laws, some because they were specifically asked to do so and some as a matter of choice. They realize that they are an important link between their children and their ex-partner's parents and they don't want their children to be robbed of that important relationship. They send photographs of their children, write letters with news of school functions and special events and encourage their children to send cards to their grandparents for special holidays.

Kornhaber and Woodward, in *Grandparents/Grandchildren—The Vital Connection,* encourage grandparents to be "the guardians of the young." They advise grandparents to "let everyone in your family know that they have you to rely on in a family emergency." Divorce, remarriage, and subsequent moves taking the children away from one parent all constitute family emergencies. Whether you choose to use your parents in that way or not, grandparents can be a tremendous resource to your children in a time of instability, uncertainty, and loss.

The main link your long-distance children have to your extended family is you. You are the one who must be committed to ensuring that your children stay in touch with your relatives. That might mean organizing a family reunion to coincide with a time your children will be with you. It might mean making a special effort to fly your children back for a big family get-together, such as a wedding, even though there is not much opportunity for relaxed visiting during such events. You can suggest to your parents that they go visit your children, if that is feasible financially and if their relations with your ex-partner are cordial enough so that they will be able to make arrangements to see the children. Or perhaps the children can go visit your parents for a week of their summer vacation. You are the one who will have to put all that in motion. The more you are involved with your long-distance children, the more you can control how much contact they have with your extended family. Many long-distance parents make sure that whenever their children visit, they also spend time with relatives. "Just about every time Tommy visits me," says Max, "he gets to visit with my mother. It's just part of what we do, and none of us would have it otherwise."

One of the most difficult aspects of remarried life with long-distance children is the jealousy and competition that arise between all members of the family. A long-distance child watching his parent form a new family complete with stepchildren and children born of that marriage always wonders where he fits in. Long-distance children wonder if there is a place for them in your home and in your heart. Your child might come for a visit, see all the new toys his stepsiblings have, and feel he's getting the short end of the stick back home with Mom.

"The greater the number of children, the greater the opportunities for jealousy and rivalry for parental affection," say Drs. Emily and John Visher, preeminent authorities on stepfamily life. Long-distance children, especially, need to deal with their feelings of being rejected or abandoned by their parent. "My dad has a new family now," says Tina, age nine. "I know he still loves me, but since he moved away, I don't get to see him much anymore." Tina thinks about her dad's new family a lot. She thinks about them in school, when she should be listening to the teacher. She imagines her dad being very happy with his new family, playing with all his new children, taking them to the park, going on bike rides together. Those are the things she used to do with her dad, when he still lived nearby.

Tina is heartbroken. Both her parents need to help Tina with these feelings. Her mother is aware of her sadness but feels she can't do anything about it, since it is her father who is rejecting her. Actually, Tina's mom has a lot to do with the situation. She makes it very difficult for Tina's father to stay in touch with his daughter. She is hostile to him when he calls and she has lied to him on occasion about Tina's whereabouts. Tina's mother needs to understand that even though she may be furious at her ex-partner, he is still Tina's father and Tina needs him. She needs to work on her own angry feelings and not interfere with Tina's relationship with her dad. When Tina grows older and learns that her mom interfered in her relationship with her dad, she will be enraged at her mother. Tina is having a difficult enough time as it is, with her dad living so far away and having another family. Her mother needs to make it easier for Tina, not harder.

Tina's father needs to be made aware of her feelings. Both parents should be in communication with each other to see if there are ways for Tina and her dad to be more involved with one another. Tina has never visited with her dad since he remarried, and she would like to. Her dad is somewhat apprehensive about this, wondering how everyone will get along, but he is willing to give it a try. Mom has to allow Tina to go, emotionally as well as physically, and dad has to grab hold of Tina and claim her as his daughter. There is much work to do.

Before a long-distance child comes to visit, a tremendous amount of anticipation and expectation builds up. Children living in the home permanently tend to resent the ''honored guest'' status that many long-distance children have. They get away with more, they are disciplined less when they come to visit, and some children feel that their parents are walking on tiptoe to please the long-distance visitor. Brooke, age fourteen, notes:

My mom goes nuts before her son comes to visit. She cooks all these fancy dishes that she never makes for us. It's like the prince is coming and we are all his ladies in waiting. I'd just as soon he stayed where he was.

It is difficult to resist the temptation to go to great lengths for a child who visits a parent only two times a year. I wouldn't even suggest to you that you do resist the temptation. As a long-distance parent, you have few opportunities to treat your child in person. But do recognize that your special favors might cause some resentment among your second family.

Children feel jealous about parental affection that they feel is shifting from them to the visiting child. Brooke, age eleven, and her stepmother have a good relationship. Brooke gets included in the plans her stepmother makes when her son comes to visit, and Brooke understands the importance of these visits to her stepmother. Yet she feels shut out and that her stepmother is paying more attention to her son that she is to Brooke. Brooke is right. Without malicious intent, her stepmother is putting Brooke aside so she can devote herself to her son. It will only be for a week, she reasons, and then she and Brooke will be close again. In the meantime, Brooke feels rejected. Her stepmother could include her more when her son is visiting, as well as before he arrives. Brooke's father could be forewarned to pay special attention to his daughter during the visit. It's a delicate balance for all of the family members to achieve.

Discuss your feelings with your family about an upcoming visit and listen to their feelings about it, as well. Explain to your family how important this visit is to you and how difficult it is for you to meet everyone's needs. Tell them that you want your long-distance-child to feel welcome and ask them to assist you in this. Ask your stepchildren what difficulties arise for them when your child visits. When they tell you, don't be quick to explain or defend yourself—just listen to them. Then they will tell you more.

When long-distance children visit, children living in the home are asked to share their bedrooms and their bathrooms, which is no small thing for an adolescent! Children are very protective of their territory, and any invasion of their space is felt acutely. They are less than thrilled about the prospects of giving up some of their room to a veritable stranger. On the other hand, the stranger—your long-distance child—knows that he is intruding and that he really doesn't have a room of his own at your house. Your stepchild is granting him two drawers in his dresser, for which he is supposed to be grateful.

Tension usually runs high in the beginning of a visit. Some families plan an outing soon after the long-distance child arrives, to get everyone out of the house and focused on an activity together. Other families like to gather everyone together to talk about expectations for the visit and things they'd like to do together. Parents can acknowledge that this is a tense time for everyone, that it will take time to get used to being together, and that you expect everyone will put their best foot forward. Set a positive tone for your family, but don't expect that they will merrily follow along!

The more often a child visits, however, the less revered his status will be and the more he should be required to fit into the everyday life of the household. It will take many visits before you get the knack of including your long-distance child in your new family. It will probably take years to do so without incurring some resentment and upset on the part of the other people who live in your house.

Remarrying means partnership in many ways, but it does not necessarily mean that you will have a partner in sharing the excitement of a visit from your child. The chances are that your new mate will think it's nice that your child is coming, but in no way will his enthusiasm match yours. You may be disappointed, but it is part of the reality of having children with whom your mate is not particularly close. You may be even more disappointed if you care for your mate's children on a daily basis and have come to feel close with them. You somehow expect these feelings will be reciprocated, that your mate will go out of his way for your children as you have done for his. That just may not be the case. Your mate is not being nasty or withholding because he is not as excited as you are about an impending visit from your child. The truth is that no one cares as much about your child as you do, except for your ex-partner. This includes your new mate. And therein lies the loneliness of the long-distance parent.

The rivalry and competition between stepsiblings also extends to competitive feelings between a parent and stepchild, whether living in the same home or many miles away. Maureen is a stepparent to Caitlin, age eleven. When Maureen married Caitlin's father, Taylor, she brought two young sons of her own to the marriage. Within a year of their marriage, Caitlin moved out of state with her mother. "Taylor and I would have gotten divorced if Caitlin had stayed in this community. She would not have been the daughter I always wanted." Maureen now feels that if Caitlin had lived with them full time, she and Caitlin might have been able to work out their relationship, but every other weekend in her household, which was Caitlin's schedule, was not good for Maureen at all. "My kids got along fine with Caitlin. It was me. I didn't look forward to her coming and I was jealous of her relationship with Taylor the whole time she was here."

It's important to examine what was going on between Maureen and Taylor that caused Maureen to feel so jealous. Maybe Taylor felt guilty about showing affection to Maureen when his daughter was present, thereby unconsciously excluding Maureen during his visitation times. Taylor might have kept Caitlin all to himself and not encouraged her to become part of the household. Perhaps he neglected his stepsons when his daughter was present, thus causing Maureen to feel angry and resentful. For her part, Maureen might have purposely stayed away from Taylor when his daughter was visiting, not wanting to compete for his affection for fear she'd lose. "We didn't have to figure all that out," said Maureen. "The fairy godmother came and took that one problem away from me.''

When Juan and Bonnie married they brought two children each from previous marriages. Bonnie's ex-husband lived five-hundred miles away and was only involved with her children when she pushed him to do so. Juan had joint custody of his two children, along with his ex-wife, who lived nearby. Bonnie found herself jealous of Juan's relationship with his children. He was the attentive father to them that neither she nor her kids had ever had. Juan did his best to include his stepchildren and his new wife in his heart, but he wondered if he had enough to go around. His kids did come first and he thought Bonnie was being immature when she got upset after he did something special for his kids. Bonnie, too, wondered what was wrong with her. She felt silly for feeling hurt so often, yet wondered why this situation was so painful for her.

What Juan and Bonnie had not yet done was to make their own relationship their first priority. They were newly married and still thought of their original families first. A remarried couple, and especially one where there are long distances between a parent and child, has an important, yet very delicate task to accomplish: to view their own relationship as central. In *Living in Step,* Roosevelt and Lofas discuss the issue of couples who seem to work out their stepfamily problems better than others. ''There seems to be a common secret to their success. The couple has put themselves first. This means that, when there's a question of priorities, each spouse understands that the needs of the couple come first.''

Long-distance parents are often hard-pressed to make decisions that look like they will have to choose between their new partners or their children, between their past and their future. Do they take some time off to see their long-lost long-distance child, or do they go away with their new partner for a much needed getaway? Is money put aside to bring the long-distance child back for a special occasion, or is that money spent on something for the new house? Do you want to indulge your long-distance child, even though your second wife thinks you're making a mistake and is angry at you about it?

Arnold and his second wife, Belinda, were arguing about Arnold's desire to fly his son Austin back from Milwaukee so they could spend Thanksgiving together. Austin was already planning to come back for Christmas and Belinda didn't think the added expense was necessary. Their conversation was at first defensive but then became more straightforward.

ARNOLD: If we were talking about spending money on your children, you wouldn't be complaining at all.

BELINDA: That's not true and you know it. And besides, their father contributes to their support. That's more than your ex-wife does.

ARNOLD: What are we really arguing about? I don't think it's about the money.

BELINDA: The truth is that I resent Austin's intrusion in our lives. He acts like a slob when he comes here, I clean up after him and then I end up resenting him and you. Can't we have one holiday that does not include your son?

ARNOLD: Are you saying that because he's a slob you don't want him to come?

BELINDA: That's part of it. The other part is that I don't have you when he's here. He has you.

Arnold went on to make two promises to Belinda in exchange for her agreeing that Austin could visit. The first was that he'd have a talk with Austin prior to his visit to discuss his habits around the house and what was required of him. In addition, Arnold agreed to do any cleaning up after his son that was necessary. The second and most important promise was that Arnold would pay special attention to Belinda during the visit and would check in with her periodically to make sure that she was feeling well taken care of. Belinda felt guilty for making it difficult for Arnold to see his only child but she knew that if she didn't tell the truth she would make the visit miserable for everyone. Austin did come to visit that Thanksgiving and was a much better-behaved child than he had been in the past. Arnold saw that he had never made any demands on his son when he visited, and when he did so, Austin complied readily. Belinda was pleased that the visit went well and found she was actually looking forward to his return over Christmas.

In the beginning years of a new marriage when relationships are often very tenuous, such deliberations may feel quite thorny. Your marriage, and the decisions you make are based on where your heart lies. Perhaps you feel guilty for feeling so happy in your new marriage while the kids are miserable being far away from you. It takes time for this kind of allegiance to shift, and sometimes it never does. But if it doesn't, if you don't make your relationship with your mate primary, then all of your children, long-distance, step, and newborn, will be caught in a morass of divided loyalties, confusion, and possible chaos. It is only out of the constancy and security of a strong marital unit that children will come to feel safe and well loved.

When a natural parent moves in order to remarry and takes a child with him, the relationship between the child and the stepparent can be even more strained. After all, the child reasons, it is because of my stepparent that my parent moved and took me away from my home. If they hadn't gotten married, Mom, Dad, and I would all still be living in the same town and I wouldn't have to go through all of this pain. "I was mad that another person was coming in between me and my dad," says Tamara, age thirteen. "We were always very close and I felt like my stepmom was taking my dad away from me." Her stepmom was also taking her away from her mom, although that was not spoken about. It has been three years now since she and her dad moved so he could remarry. She misses her mom but wouldn't want to be living with her, and she and her stepmom are doing well. "It just gets so complicated sometimes," says Tamara, "that I try not to think about it."

It *is* very complicated. Sorting out all the complex feelings that children have about their family situation is an almost impossible task. We can help children disentangle their feelings by being very sensitive to what they are experiencing and by helping them talk about it. You can assume that this kind of transition will be a difficult one for them. Tell your child that you know how hard it must be to have to leave one parent and go to a strange place to live with an even stranger family. Your child needs to know that you will do your very best to make the transition as smooth as possible for her.

Put yourself in the place of your child. What questions do you think you might have if your parent was moving to remarry and taking you away from your other parent? What feelings might you have about this auspicious event? You can assume that your child will be frightened about the upcoming move. Even though you and your ex-partner may have divorced years ago, the move will reawaken feelings of loss. The child may not want to let go of the memories she had when you all lived together as a family. The move will heighten those memories. Her familiar world will be replaced by the unknown, at least in the beginning. Your upcoming marriage will force her to confront, once again, the fantasy of you and her other parent reuniting.

- "Where will I go to school?"
- "Will I have to share a bedroom?"
- "Will I be able to ride my bike to the store?"
- "What is it like there?"
- "When will I see Mom again?"
- "Is your new wife strict?"
- "Who will be in charge of me?"

The difficulty of sorting out feelings can be exacerbated by a set of circumstances in which the child may not be close to, or identified with, the natural parent she is moving away from. The stepparent may take on a parental role and put the child in more conflict.

For instance, Tamara and her natural mother are not particularly close. They love each other, to be sure, but they are not close. The closer Tamara gets to her stepmother, the more conflict she is likely to feel about her relationship with her own mother. She might wonder why she can't have this kind of closeness with her own mom. The geographical distance makes the alienation she feels with her mom even greater. She may feel angry at her stepmom for creating this situation in the first place.

Loyalty issues, which are the central problems all children of divorce face, can be compounded for the child. Can she love two women, her mom and her stepmom? Her relationship with her long-distance mom takes on more the nature of fantasy, while her relationship with her stepmom is based more in reality. The long-distance parent is idealized and only when the child spends time with her natural mother, which may not be that often, does she get to experience the real parent.

Many factors can affect the relationship a child has with his stepparent and long-distance parent of the same sex. The age of the child at the time of the separation from the natural parent will influence his adjustment. The younger the child, the more risk there is of developing problems. The older the child, the more autonomy the child has, the more he will be able to understand his situation. The closeness of the child's relationship with the natural parent will also affect the stepparent/stepchild relationship.

The attitude of the stepparent toward the child is central to the healthy adjustment of the child. If the stepparent is in competition with the natural parent, the child will feel he has to choose between two parents. If, however, the stepparent recognizes the importance of the relationship the child has with his natural parent and encourages that relationship, the child is not forced to pick one parent over the other. Both are important and both can be included in his life.

The natural parent can also promote or sabotage the

relationship with the stepparent. Children are quick to pick up their parents' feelings. It would not even be necessary to criticize a stepparent outwardly for a child to know you do not like the stepparent, or want your child to like him.

Both parents must resolve their anger and differences in order for children to move on in their own development, which may include accepting a stepparent in their lives. A marriage may be over on paper, but the emotional warfare can go on for years. The battleground is often the children, who wouldn't even know how to go about winning the war if they tried. Minor skirmishes are often fought in the courts, with children the losers every time. Children need all the help they can get from both their parents and their stepparents to accept the changes that are taking place in their family life. Parents need to sort out their own feelings in order to be more effective in helping children with theirs.

Research about parenting practices in remarried families indicates that "children appear to accumulate rather than replace fathers, particularly when the father outside the home maintains an active presence in the child's life." Frank F. Furstenberg, Jr., and Christine Winquist Nord, in an article published in the *Journal of Marriage and the Family* entitled "Parenting Apart: Patterns of Child-rearing After Marital Disruption," speak about children having more difficulty with their stepmothers. "Children seem to find it harder to incorporate new mothers than new fathers." Usually, young children are bonded more closely with their mothers than their fathers. Therefore, a female attempting to replace that original relationship could feel like a threat to the child. Similarly, stepmothers with stepchildren living with them are more likely to be more involved in the children's lives. Stepmothers take on many of the functions of a mother and play a more active role than stepfathers do with their children.

New stepfamily relationships cannot be pushed. This is especially true for children who are living far away from their other natural parent. They need time to incorporate their new parent into their psychological life and to adapt to the role their long-distance parent will play in their lives. As in adjusting to being separated from a child, this takes time. It may be years before strained relations calm down, and in some families, they never do.

But it *is* possible, and I urge you not to give up. If your family has been having difficulty for some time accommodating to new roles and positions, get professional help. There are trained professionals who have worked with stepfamilies and are familiar with the unique sets of problems inherent in stepfamily relations. A professional counselor or therapist can help you work on the problems you and your children have, and help you sort out your own priorities and commitments. If you have been struggling along for years and things haven't gotten much better, chances are they won't without some professional guidance. Don't wait any longer. Lives are at stake.

CHAPTER 8

Keeping the Vision

Things do change. Time passing does have meaning. It had been four months since I had last seen my son. Josh visited me for a brief weekend, and I drove him to the airport. I didn't go in with him to wait for his plane to leave; I didn't even ask him to call me when he got home safely. We hugged at curbside and talked about when we'd see each other next. "I feel much better when we say good-bye and we have a definite plan to see each other again," said Josh.

I'd been home for several hours and I had not done all the work I planned to do. I felt kind of droopy, and I knew I wanted to be gentle with myself. I was not distraught, as I had been so many times after saying good-bye; I was not even extremely sad and depressed. I was just blue and I felt I had a right to be. I could have worked up a few tears, though.

Josh had accompanied me to my niece's bat mitzvah in Rockville, Maryland. The family gathered for the event, and Josh's strong sense of family made him feel that he would not miss this occasion. He was given the honor of being called to the pulpit to sing some special prayers. He and I danced together at the celebration afterward. He talked to people about attending college this fall. All day people spoke positively about the way he looked, talked, sang, danced. He made me very proud.

It is easy to start thinking about all I have missed by being apart from Josh these past four years. The thought that I have been cheated out of years of enjoying his presence on a daily basis never really goes away. Yes, I know there would have been plenty of times when parenting would have been difficult, but right now, that thought does not lift my spirits.

However, this year will bring some semblance of normality to my life. Josh will be going to college in the fall and I can finally say, when asked about him, that he is away at school. I don't have to explain that he lives with his father, tell how often I see him, how I feel about him living apart from me, and all the other endless questions that well-meaning people often ask. He's in college, I'll say glibly, and that will be the end of that.

On the other hand, maybe it won't be! If people ask me how it is now that he's in college, do I miss him and those kind of kids-going-off-to-college questions, I will mutter something about having practice in matters of this sort. Or maybe I'll just say yes, I do miss him, and leave it at that.

I can look back on the past four years and see how time passing has healed many wounds. When Josh first moved, I could not envision a time when I would stop crying. My thoughts were not on anything else but his absence or when we would see each other again. Other long-distance parents have told me about the excruciating pain they felt when their children first moved away. The pain lasts a long time and the children feel it as well.

The sense of sadness and loss is ongoing, but time does help ease it. "My son pines for his father every time he comes back home," says a custodial parent. She watches her son relive the original separation, or so it seems. "I look at his face, just hurting from being apart." What is different, though, is that her son's acute pain does not last as long as it used to. He knows that now, too, which is what helps him—and his mother—get through the night.

My own personal experience, first with being divorced and then with being a long-distance parent, combined with my professional experience, has left me with very strong opinions about the importance of keeping families together. I have experienced the trauma of dividing a family firsthand, and so has my son. I have also seen the devastation that divorce brings to countless children and adults. Therefore, in my professional work with divorcing couples, my first goal is to see if, indeed, this marriage can be saved. People have chosen each other for a reason, and that is to attempt to work out and heal the wounds of their past. Diana Adile Kirschner and Sam Kirschner, in *Comprehensive Family Therapy,* speak about marriage as an opportunity for people to "fill each other's needs for approval, affection, emotional empathy, special attention and play." Marriage can be the time when partners help each other to grow up and have their emotional needs satisfied as they never have been before.

Sometimes people have made a bad choice and divorce is the most humane solution. More often, partners are simply not aware of how to go about meeting their own and each other's emotional needs. A good therapist can help the couple understand why they chose each other in the first place, what they were seeking in a mate, and how to fill in the emotional gaps of their childhood.

When children are involved, I stress to the couple how difficult it will be for them and for their children to separate. I do not hesitate to enumerate the tremendous loss and pain children suffer when their parents separate. I cite research study after research study, pointing to the very long-lasting negative effects of divorce in children. It is the rare child who bounces back and who is not permanently scarred by the divorce in some way.

If, after working on the issues in the marriage, it becomes clear that these partners are simply not able or willing to continue being together, the next step in counseling is to prepare them and the children for the separation. Plans are made for telling the children about the impending separation. We discuss various options for custody of the children. I talk to the couple about the importance of the children having a strong, intimate relationship with both parents and stress that both parents are needed for the child to develop into an emotionally healthy adult. Very often, I assist the couple in working out their own agreement concerning shared parenting. This includes a schedule for who the children will live with and when, financial support of the children, activities the children are involved in, causes for termination of the agreement, and a plan for settling disputes that may arise in the future.

The subject of a possible move by either parent often comes up in these discussions; if it doesn't, I bring it up. I strongly urge the parent not to move. I urge people to sacrifice the important job in another city with a big pay raise. I tell them to alter their lifelong desire to live in the mountains, or the city, or in the country, or wherever they are not. What is most important at this time is to remain close to the children.

For all the positive possibilities inherent in it, long-distance parenting is the *least preferable option* to other custody arrangements, short of never seeing the children at all. One man whose newly separated wife and two-year-old-twin boys lived in Hawaii, where he and his wife had lived for many years, came to see me. He and his wife had already been through marital counseling and were ready to dissolve the marriage. Planning to move back to Philadelphia to be closer to his family and preparing to fight for custody of his sons, he asked me for my advice and if I thought his plan was a sound one. I told him he was making a big mistake. The best interests of his sons would not be served if they grew up living with one parent, whether that one parent was their father or their mother. He had a good job in Hawaii and no job prospects here. How was he planning to provide for his sons financially? Well, he said, he'd work that out. One of his main concerns was that he wanted his sons to grow up knowing his family—his parents, brothers, and other relatives. I told him that his first concern should be that his sons grow up knowing their own parents—both parents. And what if he lost his custody battle? Would he then return to Philadelphia by himself? Yes, he would, and he would have his sons come here for the summers. Any other visits would probably prove too expensive.

I strongly suggested that he go back to Hawaii and work out a joint-custody arrangement with his ex-wife. That was the best possible resolution for his boys, short of a reconciliation. They were still very young and needed many years of strong parenting ahead. He would be committing a grave injustice to his children if he did any less. He asked me for a referral to a child psychologist, to see if that person would agree with me, and I gave him one. He called me a week later to say that not only did the child psychologist tell him to go back to Hawaii, but so did another therapist he consulted. He got three professional opinions, all concurring that he belonged near his sons and his ex-wife, not thousands of miles away. He was taking a plane back to Hawaii the next day and called to thank me for pushing him to be an involved father to his children. His father had always been fairly distant with him and he had always told himself he would be a better father with his children. He was on his way home to do just that.

Whether your children live in the same community, or a hundred or a thousand miles away, there are choices you can make and actions you can take to be more involved in their lives. Is there a time you can see them that's not part of the regular schedule? How about sending them a card for no reason at all? A midweek phone call to say "I love you" is something every child wants to hear. The image of an uninvolved long-distance parent is a stereotype that needs to be broken down. Long-distance parents can be committed to their child's personal growth and take an active part in their development, although it takes creativity, imagination, and resolve to be a devoted parent despite the geographical distance.

One couple who had been separated for two years came to see me. They had a five-year-old daughter, Julia, and lived three hours apart from each other, she in the country and he in the city. They had worked out a schedule of caring for their daughter where she lived with one parent for three months, spending every other weekend with the other parent, and then they switched. The child had attended two different day care centers when she was younger and now was in two separate nursery schools. Julia was warmly welcomed back by her teacher and classmates each time she switched schools, and the situation seemed to be a good one for everyone. The only snag in the plan was that within a year, Julia would be attending first grade, and she couldn't continue switching schools any longer. Neither parent was willing to be the vacation parent. They both wanted Julia living with them for her school days. Neither parent had remarried and both had jobs they liked.

If they were truly interested in meeting Julia's needs, I told them, they would live in the same area. That way, Julia's life wouldn't be as divided between parents and she could live with them each, half the time, in the same community. The city mouse had no interest in moving to the country and the country mouse thought she'd be consumed by poisonous fumes if she moved to the city. They were truly at a stalemate as to how to go about making this very important decision. I then suggested that they both move to a third location of mutual choice. They had both grown up in the South and still had relatives there, so they talked about moving to Tennessee, where they both had some roots. The danger in doing this, of course, would be that they would be extremely dependent on one another, which would not be in their best interest. I then discovered that they talked on the phone together every night during the past two years, ostensibly to check in with Julia and to see how she was doing. I asked them if they had ever thought of reconciling. He said he had never stopped loving her; he just didn't know how to live with her anymore. She wasn't so sure about anything.

As the months went by, our work together focused on the possibility of a reconciliation. One thing that had drawn them together in the first place was their common desire to have a family and a home together. If they could still manage to do that, one of their basic needs would be met. We worked on issues that brought conflict between them—his passivity, her anger. They learned new strategies for helping each other and liked the idea of having a marriage based on a partnership. They finally decided that they would live as husband and wife again, which would be easy to accomplish legally, since they never had divorced. On Father's Day, he, the city boy, gave up his job and moved in to her little house in the country. The family was reunited; Julia would be able to attend one school starting in the fall, and the days of long-distance parenting were over.

Most conflicting marital situations do not end like this. But if there is a chance of reuniting a family, if there is a chance of getting parents to live in the same community, I will make that effort. Whatever the parenting arrangement is, I want to help parents improve the quality of their relationships with their children as well as the quantity of time spent with them.

Remember, *any* relationship with your child is better than none at all. The less a child needs to fantasize and idealize a relationship with an absent parent, the better his sense of reality will be. Children need to know both their parents. More is better. Two involved parents, wherever they live, are better than one. Seeing a child twice a year is better than once a year; once a year is better than never. Instituting regularly scheduled phone contact is better than haphazard calling. A letter a month is better than no written communication at all. And never let finances be an excuse for why your child doesn't know you.

John, whom I've written about in earlier chapters, had never been to visit his long-distance daughter in South Carolina. A business convention brought him to Charleston recently and, very hesitantly, he told his ex-wife that he would like to visit. He had a lot of concerns about going to visit his daughter in her home territory. He didn't know if he could handle it emotionally and whether he would feel too awkward seeing his ex-wife and her new husband. As it turns out, the trip was a major success. John's ex-wife and her new husband were most cordial to him, and his daughter was thrilled to finally be able to introduce her dad to her friends and to her life in the South. The best part of the trip was that it was an opening for John to be able to see his daughter more often in the future. Plans were made for his daughter to come on an unscheduled visit next month. Who knows? Perhaps John and *his* new wife will take a trip to South Carolina some day soon. John doesn't really think that's likely, but then he didn't think it likely that he would want to go to South Carolina himself, much less make that trip and enjoy it immensely.

We don't really know all that's possible in the way of relating to our long-distance children. We have ideas and notions about how it might be and especially about how our relationships with our ex-partners will be. It's one thing to have your long-distance child always visiting you, but how about a visit to her home? Think about putting yourself in your child's daily life and how you would feel about that. If you've never seen your child's school or talked to any of her teachers or seen her in a school play, this could be a unique and memorable opportunity for you.

Don't close your mind and heart to the possibility, even if you feel it's unlikely. If your relationship with your long-distance child is not what you want it to be, you need to do some serious thinking about how to go about changing it. If you feel stuck, use a friend or relative to help you brainstorm some new ways of relating to your child. Have you and your child had a heart-to-heart talk lately? It may be uncomfortable, but there really is no way around it if you want more intimacy in your relationship.

Tell your child that this long-distance business is very rough on you and that you don't always know the best way to stay in touch. Tell your child that if it's rough for you, you know it's got to be rough on him. Ask him to tell you how he feels about you being so far away. Give him the chance to tell you how much he hates it and that he hates you for moving so far away. And then, don't get defensive.

Listen to what he has to say and encourage him to say more. Then tell him how much you miss him and think about him and wish you could be together more. Tell him abut how it was with you and your dad, that you didn't get to be with your dad very much because he was so busy working, so you know how lousy he must feel. Don't hold back.

Acknowledge the reality that you *are* living apart, and that no matter what you say or do, it still will be hard and painful at times. Remind him that you want to work toward having a closer relationship and that you want your child to help you do just that. Ask him if he has any ideas about what will bring you closer together. Maybe there are things his friends do with their fathers that he would like to do with you. You might not be able to be a regular at Little League games, but the next time you are together, perhaps you can go to a major league baseball game.

Tell your child that you want to know what goes on in his daily life, how school is, and what's happening with his friends. Is there a special project your child is working on in school or in the community where you could be of assistance? Do you know an important person he could talk to in order to get some firsthand information? Do some piece of research for him. Find out what interests your child, and then use your imagination to see how you can help him. You won't know unless you ask. If your child is reluctant to talk at first you may even have to probe a bit. Be persistent; it will pay off in the form of a meaningful relationship with your child.

Plant seeds for the future. Elana, a seventeen-year-old high school senior we met in earlier chapters, has decided to attend college on the West Coast so she can be near her father. Her strong relationship with her dad over the years had everything to do with her choice. She knew the area well, had developed friends of her own there because she visited her dad so many times, and felt excited about choosing a school in her dad's hometown, which was always a second home for her as well. Tell your child that even though you are not in the same city now, you would love it if she would consider coming to college in your area. Let her know about the fine schools and how thrilled you'd be if she chose to go to one of them.

If you have been a distant long-distance parent, your child may not welcome your involvement in her life. She may be hesitant to open her heart to you if she has felt hurt by you in the past. A child's heart is nothing to toy with, so don't make an attempt to come into her life again and then disappear when it gets too difficult for you, or because something else comes up. Something else always comes up if you allow that to happen. If you are serious about wanting a better relationship with your child, sincerely apologize for neglecting her. Assure her you will not disappear again.

Alan, whom we met in Chapter 1, neglected his children while he was still living with them, and then for years after he and his wife divorced. When his children were eighteen and twenty, he decided he wanted to make amends for his earlier mistakes and attempt to forge a new relationship with them. The older child clearly rejected his renewed interest in her. The younger daughter, however, was a bit more open, if hesitant. Gwen, now twenty, remembers clearly when her father left town.

He kind of became a hermit. He didn't talk to me and my sister and he stopped talking to his own parents, too. I never knew why he didn't get in touch with us. I guess I just decided he didn't care.

Years later, she and her sister flew to visit their father for a weekend. Gwen remembers to this day an incident in the airport in which her father was stopped by a religious solicitor.

My father totally blew up at him. He could have just ignored the guy and said, "No, thank you," but instead, he made a big scene. I remember deciding to be real good during that visit. I wasn't going to give my father any reason to blow up at *me*.

Gwen started visiting her father more often, but for some reason her older sister didn't come. She lived with her father and his second wife for a while, but that didn't work out. Neither did her father's second marriage. Her relationship with her dad became very distant once again. It's only now, when Gwen is on her own, that she and her dad are starting to have a decent relationship.

I'll never let things get so bad again between me and my father. He's really the only family I have because my mother and I aren't close at all. And my sister is a hermit herself.

Alan and Gwen are both committed to repair the damage done to their relationship in the past. They know they have both missed out on many years when they could have been closer. Alan had allowed difficult circumstances to prevent him from being the kind of father he always wanted to be and had never had himself.

Many parents today, Alan included, tell of being virtual strangers to their own parents, especially to their fathers. Samuel Osherson, in *Finding Our Fathers,* speaks of the longing men have as adults to know who their fathers were. Much is being written today regarding the mistakes many men made in being absent from family life for so many years, whether they were away at work or away at war. Children have suffered from not having the male influence in their lives and as adults still search for what Osherson calls the wounded father within.

Even though you may be far away geographically, you needn't be far away emotionally. Don't make the same mistakes that your father might have made. Being a parent is one of the primary experiences of life, one that should be treated with the utmost respect. Learn from your past mistakes and those of your parents and rededicate yourself to a different, vastly improved relationship with your child.

There is a never-ending bond between parent and child. Even if you have not been in touch for years, you are still linked together, and you always will be. Don't give up. You may be rebuffed by your child, you may be told not to call, but still, don't give up. Try again next week, next month. Try in a different way. Send a card, write a letter expressing your regrets about your previous behavior and how you want things to change.

Otto, who abandoned his girlfriend eleven years ago when she was pregnant with their child, makes no excuses for himself. "I was wrong," he says. He saw his son once, when he was two years old. As a result of work done in therapy, Otto made contact with his former girlfriend and his son, Van. It was part of a long process for Otto of claiming the child he abandoned so many years ago. He has asked for forgiveness and is making reparations for the years gone by. Van was wary, at first, and received his father's overtures with much hesitation. But during this past year of reuniting, Van has visited his father several times and they speak and write to each other regularly. Van has come to see that his father is sincere, and he is thrilled to have a father of his own.

You never know what the future will bring. Many long-distance children experience a sense of coming home when a previously absent parent wants to have a relationship with them—that is, they return to their long-distance parent in some way. There is a need to complete the relationship, to make up in some way for time lost in the past.

Even if there is only a thread left to the relationship, many children want the chance to know their parent. If he has any attachment at all to the long-distance parent, a child sometimes wants to move to be with that parent as he matures. This often comes as a shock to the custodial parent, who has raised a child, but it is understandable when the longing the child has to know his other parent is considered. A child's desire to move to be with a long-distance parent is especially strong if there is a close bond between parent and child. Boys want to be with their fathers; girls want to be with their mothers. Although such moves are not always possible, the yearning is always there.

Even when such moves are possible, it's important to remember that it is often a major change in lifestyle to have a child come to live with you when he is an adolescent. Adolescence is a difficult time in and of itself, and when you add to it the tumult of moving—a major life transition for parent and child—this time can be an upheaval in everyone's lives. But if you think of your purpose as achieving a strong, intimate relationship with your child, one in which you strive to be the parent you always wanted to be and wanted to have, and you are committed to having that kind of relationship, then you will do whatever it takes to achieve that vital parent-child bond.

For long-distance parents whose children are still young, *now* is the time to make your relationships better. If you are not getting along with your ex-partner and he makes seeing your children an uphill task, ask yourself what you can do to make a dent in that situation. Get some help: Ask your trusted friends or relatives for advice; join a support group for long-distance parents or for divorced parents; seek the advice of a professional therapist or counselor; call a lawyer experienced in these matters. Find out about the Uniform Child Custody Jurisdiction Act, which prevents kidnapping and allows for the registration of out-of-state custody orders. If your ex-partner lives in a different state and doesn't live up to her end of the custody agreement you signed, you have legal recourse in the state you live in. Apprise yourself of your legal rights. Whatever you do, do something. Time is slipping by, your child wonders why you don't see each other, and still nothing changes. That is not good enough anymore.

If you can project yourself ten years into the future, would you have any regrets about the present? Will you regret that you didn't reach out more to your long-distance children? Perhaps you would feel that your priorities were misguided, that you should have planned more vacation time to be with your children. Your children may be off at college leading their own lives, and you might regret that you really didn't have much influence over them when they were younger. Try looking back. Do what you can do now to eliminate as many of those potential regrets as possible.

None of the long-distance parents I interviewed *wanted* to be long-distance parents. Most of them expressed great sadness and pain at being apart from their children and wished they were living closer. Yet they are steadfast in their commitment to be emotionally close to their children, despite the distance. Vicki and her son, Gabe; John and his daughter, Vanessa; Cliff and Isabelle—there are many examples of parents and children who have maintained and strengthened their connection to one another even though they live apart. None of them knew how they would accomplish this when they first separated. All they knew was that they would keep the bond between them, somehow. The strong relationship that my son and I have had over the years has not been diminished by distance. Our relationship has been strengthened and nurtured and honored in a way that I did not know was possible.

As the years have gone by, many long-distance parents have made memories with their children. They have accumulated many shared experiences to draw on in their conversations and letters later on. Making memories together is what deepens their relationships and broadens areas that they share together. They can look at an event with their children and remember how it was for them together.

As a long-distance parent, keep the vision of a close, loving relationship with your child in mind. Keep looking at the big picture and at what is best for your children. Your intention to know your children and have them know you requires firm resolve. Yes, you will waver and wonder if you are doing the right thing; sometimes you will make mistakes. But if you have decided that your relationship with your children is central to your life, and you act accordingly, then you *will* be central in their lives. You will be rewarded by watching your children grow into healthy adults, and your life and theirs will be filled with intimacy and love.

Organizations and Support Groups

American Association for Marriage and Family Therapists
1717 K. Street N.W., Suite 407
Washington, D.C. 20036
(202) 429-1825
For advice in choosing a therapist.

Child Custody Evaluation Services of Philadelphia, Inc.
Box 202
Glenside, PA 19038
(215) 576-0177
Ken Lewis, Ph.D., Director
This organization runs a unique Children's Fund, which provides free transportation for long-distance parents and children to visit one another, when financially eligible.

Fathers' and Children's Equality (FACE)
P.O. Box 117
Drexel, Hill, PA 19026
(215) 688-4748
Check to see if there is a FACE chapter in your area.

Fathers of America
P.O. Box 3075
Santa Monica, CA 90403

Joint Custody Association
10606 Wilkins Avenue
Los Angeles, CA 90024
(213) 475-5352
James A. Cook, President

Mothers Without Custody
P.O. Box 56762
Houston, TX 77256-6762
Write for information regarding a support group in your area.

Parents Without Partners
7910 Woodmont Avenue, Suite 1000
Bethesda, MD 20814

Stepfamily Association of America, Inc.
602 East Joppa Road
Baltimore, MD 21204
(301) 823-7570

Bibliography

Adler, Robert E. *Sharing The Children: How to Resolve Custody Problems and Get on with Your Life.* Bethesda, MD: Adler & Adler, 1988.

Ahrons, Constance R. and Roy H. Rodgers. *Divorced Families: A Multidisciplinary Developmental View.* New York: W.W. Norton, 1987.

Burns, Cherie. *Stepmotherhood: How to Survive Without Feeling Frustrated, Left Out or Wicked.* New York: Times Books, 1985.

Furstenberg, Frank F. Jr., and Christine Winquist Nord. "Patterns of Childrearing After Marital Disruption." *Journal of Marriage and the Family.* November 1985, pp. 893–904.

Galper, Miriam. *Joint Custody and Co-Parenting. Sharing Your Child Equally.* Philadelphia: Running Press, 1980.

Gilligan, Carol. *In a Different Voice.* Cambridge, Mass: Harvard University Press, 1982.

Greif, Geoffrey L., and Mary S. Pabst. *Mothers Without Custody.* Lexington, Mass: Lexington Books, 1988.

Isaacs, Marla Beth, Braulio Montalvo, and David Abelsohn. *The Difficult Divorce. Therapy for Children and Families.* New York: Basic Books, Inc., 1986.

184 LONG-DISTANCE PARENTING

Kirschner, Diana Adile, and Sam Kirschner. *Comprehensive Family Therapy. An Integration of Systemic and Psychodynamic Treatment Models.* New York; Brunner/Mazel, 1986.

Kornhaber, Arthur and Kenneth L. Woodward. *Grandparents/Grandchildren: The Vital Connection.* New York: Anchor Press (Doubleday), 1981.

Leonard, Linda Schierse. *The Wounded Women.* Boston: Shambhala Publications, Inc., 1982.

Newman, George. *101 Ways to Be a Long Distance Super-Dad.* Mountain View, California: Blossom Valley Press, 1984 (To order, write Blossom Valley Press, P.O. Box 4044, Blossom Valley Station, Mountain View, CA 94040.)

Osherson, Samuel. *Finding Our Fathers: The Unfinished Business of Manhood.* New York: The Free Press, 1986.

Ricci, Isolina. *Mom's House, Dad's House: Making Shared Custody Work.* New York: Macmillan Publishing Co., 1980.

Roosevelt, Ruth, and Jeannette Lofas. *Living in Step, A Remarriage Manual for Parents and Children.* New York: McGraw Hill, 1976.

Visher, Emily B., and John S. Visher. *Stepfamilies: A Guide to Working with Stepparents & Stepchildren.* New York: Brunner/Mazel, 1979.

Wallerstein, Judith S., and Joan Berlin Kelly. *Surviving the Breakup: How Children and Parents Cope with Divorce.* New York: Basic Books, Inc., 1980.

Ware, Ciji. *Sharing Parenthood after Divorce.* New York: The Viking Press, 1982.

Further Readings

Einstein, Elizabeth. *The Stepfamily: Living, Loving & Learning*. Boston: Shambhala Publications, Inc., 1985

Fisher, Roger, and William Ury. *Getting to Yes: Negotiating Agreement without Giving in*. New York: Penguin Books, 1981.

Gardner, Richard A. *The Parents Book about Divorce*. New York: Bantam Books, 1980.

——— *The Boys' and Girls' Book about Divorce*. New York: Bantam Books, 1971.

Krementz, Jill. *How It Feels When Parents Divorce*. New York: Alfred A. Knopf, 1988.

Lansky, Vicki. *Vicki Lansky's Divorce Book for Parents*. New York: New American Library, 1989.

Paskowicz, Patricia. *Absentee Mothers*. New York: Universe Books, 1982.

Sifford, Darrell, *Father and Son*. Philadelphia: Bridgebooks, 1982.

Virtue, Doreen. *My Kids Don't Live with Me Anymc* Minneapolis: CompCare Publishers, 1988.

Visher, Emily B., and John S. Visher. *How to W Stepfamily*. New York: Dember Books, 1982.

Walker, Glynnis. *Solomon's Children: Exploding the Myths of Divorce*. New York: Arbor House, 1986.

Walker, Jan. *Parenting from a Distance: Your Rights and Responsibilities*. Danville, Ill: The Interstate Printers and Publishers, Inc., 1987.

Wheeler, Michael. *Divided Children: A Legal Guide for Divorcing Parents*. New York: W.W. Norton, 1980.

Woolley, Persia. *The Custody Handbook*. New York: Summit Books, 1979.

Index